"Relationships are fundamental to life and to making a positive impact on others. Dr. Merritt enlightens with his wisdom and teaches with his knowledge about the steps to building better relationships. Don't just read it; put his advice into practice!"

S. TRUETT CATHY
Founder and Chairman, Chick-fil-A, Inc.

"How to Be a Winner and Influence Anybody is a valuable tool to have on the journey toward 'sweet success.' In a world where accomplishment and influence are often measured by the absence of failure and the things we acquire, James Merritt refocuses our eyes and hearts using a power principle from God's Word—the fruit of the Spirit. This book pinpoints ways to find fulfillment and purpose in your life by showing ways to establish meaningful relationships with others."

JOHN C. MAXWELL
Founder, The INJOY Group

"Dr. James Merritt spoke to our football team prior to our game against Georgia Tech in 2001. He is a tremendous communicator, and I can see why he is an expert on relationships. In this book, he talks about many types of important relationships, including the most important relationship a person can have—that with Jesus Christ."

MARK RICHT
Head Football Coach, University of Georgia

"Dr. James Merritt has written a classic. I am a compulsive reader of success, inspirational, and motivational books. They don't get any better than this one!"

PAT WILLIAMS
Senior Vice President, Orlando Magic

How to
Be a
Winner
and
Influence
Anybody

How to Be a Winner

and

Influence Anybody

THE FRUIT OF
THE SPIRIT AS THE
ESSENCE OF
LEADERSHIP

JAMES MERRITT

FOREWORD BY ZIG ZIGLAR

BROADMAN
& HOLMAN
PUBLISHERS

Nashville, Tennessee

0-8054-2429-6

Published by Broadman & Holman Publishers,
Nashville, Tennessee

Subject Heading: LEADERSHIP

Except where noted differently, all New Testament
Scriptures are from the Holman Christian Standard Bible,
© 2000 by Holman Bible Publishers. All Old Testament
verses are from the New King James Version, © 1979,
1980, 1982, Thomas Nelson, Inc., Publishers.

1 2 3 4 5 6 7 8 9 10 06 05 04 03 02

This book is dedicated to

TERESA

The love of my life who made me a
Winner when she married me and is the
Greatest influence on my life.

Contents

Foreword

You meet some people and instinctively bond with them. Dr. James Merritt was one of those people for me. His heart and mind work together so beautifully that I felt a confidence in and closeness to him from the moment we said hello. As you read *How to Be a Winner and Influence Anybody*, you will understand completely what I mean because his words will touch you as his persona touched me.

Because he is an outstanding Bible student, this book is theologically sound. But what makes it so effective and applicable to everyday life is that he also teaches common sense applications that are psychologically and physiologically sound. His "fruit of the Spirit" approach to all of life will help you bear fresh fruit in your life. Since our relationships—good or bad—determine whether our influence will be positive or negative, this fruit of the Spirit approach will, when applied, enable you to make your influence positive.

How to Be a Winner and Influence Anybody is written to ease the pressures of today's high-tech/high-stress, low-touch lifestyles, and its lessons are timeless. The advice

Dr. Merritt offers is practical, down to earth, and filled with good ol' common sense and wisdom for those of us seeking happiness, joy, and contentment from life. He enables the reader to understand and appreciate why the joy of giving far outweighs the experience of receiving. This is a book about life values—goodness, faithfulness, hope, love, honor—the principles upon which you can build a marriage, a career, a business, a profession, many friendships, and so forth.

James Merritt writes with gentleness and thought-fulness as he touches on much of life's meaning, but the heart and soul of his message is to help you become a reflection of Jesus Christ. I believe you will benefit, as I did, from reading and applying the truths and principles in *How to Be a Winner and Influence Anybody.*

ZIG ZIGLAR

Author/Motivational Teacher

Acknowledgments

When a person writes a book, there may be only one author but there are many behind-the-scenes people who make the work possible.

First, I would like to thank Broadman & Holman for seeing this project through. They were so understanding in deadline extensions necessary because of the duty of being the president of the Southern Baptist Convention, as well as pastoring a church and trying to be a husband and father.

Then I would like to thank my editor, Steve Halliday. He is one of the best in the business and is both a challenge and a joy to work with.

I would like to thank Joanne Wardell, my administrative assistant, for all the help she gives me as well as the joy of working with her for sixteen years.

I want to thank my sainted mother, "Mim," who always believed in me and made me feel like a winner all of my life.

I want to thank the Fellowship of Joy, my beloved church who I love as a shepherd loves the sheep, for the joy of being their pastor—they have made me look like a winner!

I want to thank my wife Teresa and my precious sons—James, Jonathan, and Joshua—for putting up with me even when I don't always act like a winner. Being her husband and their father are the greatest privileges of my life. They are all winners in my book—literally and figuratively.

Finally, I praise and thank the dear Lord Jesus whose gift of eternal life has made me a permanent winner. Praise God for His unsearchable riches!

Becoming the Winner You Were Meant to Be

Imagine that you have just been told you have only a few days to live. No chance the prognosis was wrong; no chance the files were mixed up; no cure; no antidote; no treatment. Nothing. You have just been given the pink slip of life. Your ticket for the train to eternity has just been punched, and you will be at the station on time.

May I suggest that, at that moment, the most important thing in your life will not be the bottom line of your balance sheet, the size of your portfolio, the number of people who reported to you, the title you carried at your company, the size of your retirement pension, or the "Dr." or "Mr." in front of your name. The one thing that will leap to the top of your priority list will be *relationships*.

A recent Harris Poll asked many Americans to name what they considered most important in life. Consider their response:

- relationships (56 percent)
- religious faith (21 percent)
- making the world a better place (12 percent)
- a fulfilling career (5 percent)
- money (5 percent)[1]

Those polled rated relationships as more important than either career or money by a ratio of more than *ten to one*. While it could be debated that not everyone in the survey responded truthfully, at least the poll reveals the core of what, deep down, people know is truly important. Consider how crucial relationships are to everyone:

- A successful marriage depends upon the *relationship* between the husband and the wife.
- A happy home depends upon the *relationship* between the parents and the children (and between the siblings).
- A prosperous business depends upon the *relationship* between the employees and the customers.
- A peaceful community depends upon the *relationship* between the neighbors.
- A successful political campaign depends upon the *relationship* between the candidate and the voters.
- A stable nation depends upon the *relationship* between the government and its citizens.
- World peace depends upon the *relationship* between nations.
- One's eternal destiny depends upon a personal *relationship* with Jesus Christ.

John Donne was right: "No man is an island, entire of itself; every man is a piece of the continent, a part of the main . . . any man's death diminishes me, because I am involved in mankind; and therefore never send to know for whom the bell tolls; it tolls for thee."[2]

To put simply what Donne put so profoundly, even the Lone Ranger was not so lone—he had Tonto. Variety may give life spice, but *relationships* give life significance, purpose, and meaning. This book will address the key to happy, productive relationships.

All kinds of books discuss the "how" of relationship building; this book deals with the "who." And that who is *you*. No one on earth has the power to influence the people you know more than you do. *Who you are matters more than what you do.*

Over the last several years, a debate has raged in this country over whether character counts, especially in leadership. The consensus appears to be that a person's behavior in private has little bearing on his or her ability to lead or influence in public.

I strongly disagree.

I believe a core of character exists within us that, if activated and lived out, enables us not only to have maximum inner peace and joy but also to achieve the greatest possible impact on others. Jesus, the greatest Man who ever walked the earth, once said, "By their fruit, you shall know them."

What if your life bore fruit day in and day out? By "fruit" I don't mean apples or pears; I mean love, joy, peace, patience, kindness, goodness, faithfulness, gentleness, and self-control. Would you be happier, less stressed, easier to follow, and more influential with others?

What if your boss, your spouse, your children, and your friends were to manifest this fruit as well? How different would your marriage be? Your family? Your business?

In his best-selling book *How to Win Friends and Influence People,* Dale Carnegie quoted John Rockefeller as saying that "the ability to deal with people is as purchasable a commodity as sugar or coffee, and I will pay more for that ability than any other under the sun."[3]

Rockefeller's words still ring true today. Who you are in the core of your being and how you relate to others will be more valuable at the end of life's journey than the political acumen of a Bill Clinton, the wealth of a Ted Turner, the fame of a Muhammad Ali, or the influence of a Michael Jordan.

I believe God created all of us with the possibility of becoming winners—successful men and women who wield an unbelievably positive impact on those around us. The key is making sure that we bear the right fruit— the kind of fruit that the best-selling book in history calls the "fruit of the Spirit."

I hope this book will help you go where the God-given seed within you can be cultivated and watered so that it blossoms, making you into the winner God wants you to be. Believe me, when this happens, you can influence almost anybody in an overwhelmingly positive way.

If You're Not Loving, You're Not Living

In German it is *Ich liebe Dich.*
In French it is *Je t'aime.*
In Mandarin it is *Wo ai ni.*
In Dutch it is *Ik hou van jou.*
In Japanese it is *Sukiyo.*
In Lebanese it is *Bahibak.*
In Russian it is *Ya tyebya lyublyu.*
In Italian it is *Ti amo.*
In Greek it is *S'agapo.*
In Spanish it is *Te amo.*
In Polish it is *Kocham cie.*
In Hawaiian it is *Aloha au ia'oe.*
In Lithuanian it is *Myliu tave.*
In Romanian it is *Te iubesc.*[1]

> *Love in your heart wasn't put there to stay; love isn't love till you give it away.*

What is "it"? In any language, it is the most powerful expression of the most powerful emotion and experience in the world. It, of course, is "I love you." An old song says, "You're nobody till somebody loves you." If that is true, then everybody is somebody because God loves everybody.

You Can't Lose When You Love

This book describes the character qualities that will make anybody a winner and maximize your potential influence on anybody. It is no coincidence that we begin our training with love. No lover is ever a loser (I mean "lover" in a nonsexual sense). We *never* lose when we love.

But the question is, What do we mean by "love"?

If you were to ask who the greatest lover in the history of the world is, I strongly suspect that Jesus Christ would win, hands down. He preached love and He practiced love. This man gave in one single statement the greatest explanation of love ever recorded. In doing so, He informed us that love is three-dimensional.

Love Has an Upward Dimension

Jesus opened our eyes to the true nature of love in Matthew 22:35–40: "And one of them, an expert in the law, asked a question to test Him: 'Teacher, which command-ment in the law is the greatest?' [Jesus] said to him, '"You shall love the Lord your God with all your heart, with all your soul, and with all your mind." This is the greatest and most important commandment. The second is like it: "You shall love your neighbor as yourself." All the Law and the Prophets depend on these two commandments.'"

In this passage the Lord Jesus reveals three directions for love: toward God, others, and ourselves. The first love—for God—is an upward love that must take priority. We should love God *first*. Jesus tells us that God deserves *all* of our love, not only *part* of our love. We should love no one more than we love God.

Jesus plainly taught that God, in His love, created human beings. Life does not precede love; love precedes life. Indeed, "God is love" (1 John 4:8). It is the love of God that gave us life in creation and in salvation, so any attempt to talk of true love apart from God would short-change both the meaning of the term and its source.

Jesus taught that if love is to be fully manifested, maximally beneficial, and mutually satisfying, we should love God (first), others (second), and ourselves (last). Jesus' command for us to love clues us in about the true nature and behavior of love. First, love cannot be merely emotional—only a matter of feelings. Teenage love has been described as a feeling you feel when you feel that what you feel is a feeling you have never felt before. That may be an accurate depiction of juvenile ardor, but genuine love is more than a mere feeling.

Love is also a matter of the will. *Love is a commandment followed by a commitment.* Although feelings are important, true love functions regardless of feelings. Perhaps an illustration will show what I mean. For thousands of years (and to this day in some Eastern cultures), parents arranged the majority of marriages. In some cases, the bride and bridegroom never saw each other until their wedding day.

A certain young lady from India was to be married to a young man she had never met. One day she received a letter from her fiancé to acquaint them with each other prior to the wedding. But the young woman returned the letter unopened, saying she believed love should be developed after marriage and not before.

In explaining her stance, the woman said, "When we are born, we cannot choose our mother and father or our brothers and sisters. Yet we learn to live with them and to love them. So it is with our husband or wife."

In societies that accept such a philosophy, divorce is almost nonexistent. While I do not suggest that we return to the practice of arranged marriages, I do insist that "romantic love" as popularly understood has little to do with a successful marriage. Love is more than feelings.

So is it possible to love others or to experience love apart from God? Certainly, for people do it every day. But if Jesus was right, unless one first loves God and receives His love, it is impossible to experience or manifest the greatest love as fully as possible. If you love God, your love for others will grow even greater, for this upward love supernaturally produces a love for others.

In fact, when you love God the most, you will love others the best. British author C. S. Lewis once said, "When I have learned to love God better than my earthly dearest, I shall love my earthly dearest better than I do now."

Love Has an Outward Dimension

Jesus also calls us to love our neighbor. A love for God inescapably motivates a love for others. Of course, it's hard to love everybody. As C. W. Vanderbergh wrote, "To love the whole world for me is no chore. My only real problem is my neighbor next door."

Most businesses would benefit greatly if the boss truly loved his employees and they knew it. Most marriages would be happier if spouses heard and saw constant reminders that they were loved. Most families would be happier if the parents constantly and lovingly affirmed their children.

Consider two simple but extremely powerful principles that can transform any relationship almost overnight. Here's the first: *When it comes to love, say it.*

My dad went to heaven almost a year and a half before I wrote this book. He grew up in a relatively good—but loveless—home. Between them, my grandparents lived a total of 180 years. In the combined 106 years my dad knew them, they never once told him they loved him. I am so glad that the last time I saw my dad alive, I told him, "You are my best man and I love you."

About thirteen years ago I met a Palestinian named Tony who has since become part of my family. Until I told him "I love you," he had never heard another man say those three words to him. At first, all he could say was "thank you." I just kept on speaking those three words. After years of telling him, he said to me, "I love you, man." Later he told me that he has never felt so good about expressing his love to others in such an open way.

I can name at least four reasons why those three words need to come from our lips regularly and often: (1) you need to say it; (2) you need to hear yourself say it; (3) others need to hear you say it; and (4) you need to hear it from others.

What's wrong with a general telling his troops he loves them? Why doesn't a boss tell his employees he loves them? Why shouldn't a coach tell his players he loves them? In 1999, Duke University played the University of Connecticut for the NCAA men's basketball championship. Duke had a chance to win, but in the last five seconds a Duke player lost the ball and, with it, the game.

What did coach Mike Kryzewski say after he lost for the fourth time in a national championship game? "I'm really proud of my team," he declared. "I really love these guys. I have a hard time being sad. I don't coach for winning. I coach for relationships."[2]

That is one reason why Coach Kryzewski is considered one of the outstanding coaches and recruiters in America.

Husbands, your wife needs to hear you say those three words, repeatedly, every day. Don't be like the husband and wife who were sitting on a swing one afternoon. The woman turned to her spouse and said, "You never tell me you love me." Without looking at his wife, the man dryly replied, "I told you thirty-seven years ago that I loved you, and if I change my mind, I will let you know."

Men, they may *know* it, but they still need to *hear* it.

The second relationship-transforming principle is, *When it comes to love, show it.*

Love must not only be articulated but demonstrated. In the great "love chapter" of the Bible, 1 Corinthians 13, the apostle Paul constantly says, "Love is . . . love does. Love is not . . . love does not." Love is proactive, practical, and personal. It is tangible—something to be seen as well as heard.

A simple touch can convey an incredible sense of love, affirmation, and acceptance. A study conducted at UCLA several years ago found that to maintain physical and emotional health, men and women need eight to ten meaningful touches each day.[3] These researchers defined meaningful touch as a gentle tap, stroke, kiss, or hug, given by a "significant other" such as a husband, wife, parent, or close friend.

Of course, in a professional relationship (and in certain personal relationships), caution should be exercised in touching anyone of the opposite sex. The point is, there is a place and a need for tangible expressions of love.

An old commercial appropriately asked parents, "Have you hugged your kids today?" Good coaches high-five their players; good husbands hug their wives; and good bosses give employees encouraging pats on the back as a way of expressing loving affirmation.

Dr. Dolores Kreiger, professor of nursing at New York University, has made numerous studies on the effect of human touch. She found that both the toucher and the one being touched receive great physiological benefit. Here's how: Red blood cells carry a substance called hemoglobin, which carries oxygen to the body's tissues. Dr. Kreiger found that hemoglobin levels in the bloodstreams of both people increase when one lays hands on the other. As hemoglobin levels rise, body tissues receive more oxygen. This oxygen increase invigorates both parties and can even aid in the healing process (the healing power of love in action).[4] An incredible true-to-life story illustrates the power of a loving touch.

Leprosy patients feel no physical pain except in the very early stages of the disease. But that lack of feeling is the problem, for after leprosy bacilli deaden nerve cells, patients lose pain as an all-important danger signal. They may step on a rusty nail or scratch an infected spot on the eyeball without even knowing it. The result can be the loss of a limb or vision, but at no point does the leprosy patient actually hurt.

Although they do not feel physical pain, leprosy patients do suffer incredibly from the rejection of the outside world. Dr. Paul Brand, a leprosy specialist, tells of a very bright young man he treated in India. In the course of his examination, he laid his hand on the patient's shoulder and informed him through a translator about the treatment he would receive. To the doctor's shock, the man began to tremble and sob uncontrollably. Brand immediately asked the translator what he had done wrong. She quizzed the patient and explained, "No, doctor. He says he is crying because you put your hand around his shoulder. Until he came here, no one had as much as touched him in many years."[5]

Lovers are winners. Lovers not only win, they make others feel like winners too. Losers refuse to love.

In the 1920s, a very interesting case came before the Massachusetts state courts. A man had been walking along a pier when he tripped over a rope and fell into the icy waters of the bay. He came up sputtering, crying for help, then sank beneath the waves. He could not swim, nor could he stay afloat. Some friends heard his cry but were too far away to help. Only a few yards away lay a young man, sunbathing on a blanket. This man was an excellent swimmer and clearly heard the drowning man cry for help.

Tragically, the sunbather did nothing. He looked on with indifference as the man sank for the final time. The family of the deceased sued the sunbather but lost when the court reluctantly ruled that the man on the blanket had no *legal* responsibility or obligation to try to rescue the drowning man.[6]

Indifference and inaction may not be illegal, but in a real sense, failure to show love is inexcusable, if not immoral. The greatest teacher on love said that love is more than an inclination; it is a demonstration: "No one has greater love than this, that someone would lay down his life for his friends" (John 15:13). It can be argued that while no one has the legal obligation to love anyone, the failure to demonstrate love is certainly immoral, for love is to be both verbally expressed and tangibly demonstrated.

Love sets off a divine chain reaction. Love is the spark that kindles the fire of compassion. Compassion is the fire that lights the candle of service. Service is the candle that ignites the torch of hope. Hope is the torch that lights the beacon of faith. Faith is the beacon that reflects the power of God. And God is the power that creates the miracle of love.

The law says, "What's mine is mine; I'll keep it."

Our lust says, "What's yours is mine; I'll take it."

True love says, "What's mine is yours; I'll share it."

The way of love is not only the right way, it is the best way. You can experience nothing as gratifying to yourself or as encouraging to others as loving others through both words and deeds.

Love Has an Inward Dimension

Many forget that Jesus said we should love our neighbors as ourselves (Matt. 22:39). On the surface, this seems to be a mandate for self-love. But when we consider His words in context, we see the principle Jesus gave was both radically new and refreshing. Put simply, Jesus declared that when we love God the way we ought to love God, we will love others the way we ought to love others; and when we love God and others the way we should, we will love ourselves in a proper and healthy way.

Love can give you a healthy mental picture of yourself, enhancing the type of self-esteem that avoids self-worship or self-idolization. The great Swiss psychologist Paul Tournier once said, "If a person will love God the way he ought to love God, he will then love others the way he ought to love others; and when he loves God and others the way they ought to be loved, he will never need a psychiatrist."

The topics of self and self-esteem have generated an incredible amount of press over the last several years. Much of the coverage has been counterproductive, fostering an unhealthy obsession with self and spawning a culture of selfishness that chants the mantra of "What's in it for me?" It is not enough to affirm that "I'm OK and you're OK," for neither person may really be OK. But if you are OK with God and OK with others, chances are you will be OK with yourself. When you love God and your neighbor, self won't seem so important. You will find that love can motivate in a way that fame or fortune never could.

Evangeline Booth, daughter of the founder of the Salvation Army, sat in a squalid slum one day, cleaning the sores of a drunk woman. "I wouldn't do that for a million dollars," said a friend.

"Neither would I," replied Ms. Booth.

Love Gives Life to Living

Henry Drummond once said:

> To love abundantly is to live abundantly; and to love forever is to live forever. Hence, eternal life is inextricably bound up with love. We want to live forever for the same reason we want to live tomorrow. Why do you want to live tomorrow? It is because there is someone who loves you, and whom you want to see tomorrow and be with and love back. There is no other reason why we should live on than that we love and we are loved. It is when a man has no one to love him, or thinks that he has no one to love him, that he commits suicide. So long as

he has friends, those who love him and whom he loves, he will live; because to live is to love.[7]

Drummond was right. If you are not loving, you are not living. Even the poorest person on earth can give away love. We all need to be loved and we all need to love someone else, for there is always someone who needs our love.

Why not start now to become a loving person or a person better at loving? For the next thirty days, try the following:

- Tell every member of your family that you love them and give them several loving touches, pats, hugs, and kisses every day.
- If you are a boss, manager, or employer, tell your employees that you love and appreciate them for the work they do. Find some way to give a tangible expression (note, card, or pat on the back) of your loving affirmation.
- If you are an employee, do the same for your employers.
- If you have been at odds with someone, go to that person and affirm your love for him, regardless of your differences.

One word of warning: loving others and expressing that love verbally and tangibly can entail great risk. But that is the difference between losers and winners: *A winner is willing to risk not being like others to rise above others.* A poem about risk says it so well:

Risks
To laugh is to risk appearing the fool.
To weep is to risk appearing sentimental.

To reach out for another is to risk involvement.

To expose feelings is to risk exposing your true self.

To place your ideas, your dreams, before a crowd is to risk their loss.

To love is to risk not being loved in return.

To live is to risk dying.

To hope is to risk despair.

To try is to risk failure.

But risks must be taken, because the greatest hazard in life is to risk nothing.

The person who risks nothing, does nothing, has nothing, and is nothing.

They may avoid suffering and sorrow, but they cannot learn, feel, change, grow, love, live.

Chained by their attitudes, they are slaves, they have forfeited freedom.

Only the person who risks is free.[8]

A Tidal Wave of Joy

Love involves risk, pain, and heartache but can bring a tidal wave of joy that washes the tough times away.

David Ireland wrote *Letters to an Unborn Child* while dying from a crippling neurological disease. He wrote these letters to the unborn child still in the womb of his wife—a child he knew he might never see, hold, rock, kiss, or take to a ball game or a movie. A child he might never shoot baskets with, take to the circus, or comfort after a bad dream. He desperately wanted that child to know that, whether dead or alive, "Daddy loves his son or daughter." With that in mind, David wrote the following:

Your mother is very special. Few men know what it's like to receive appreciation for taking their wives out to dinner when it entails what it does for us. It means that she has to dress me, shave me, brush my teeth, comb my hair, wheel me out of the house and down the steps, open the garage and put me in the car, take the pedals off the chair, stand me up, sit me in the seat of the car, twist me around so that I'm comfortable, fold the wheelchair, put it in the car, go around to the other side of the car, start it up, back it out, get out of the car, pull the garage door down, get back into the car, and drive off to the restaurant.

And then, it starts all over again; she gets out of the car, unfolds the wheelchair, opens the door, spins me around, stands me up, seats me in the wheelchair, pushes the pedals out, closes and locks the car, wheels me into the restaurant, then takes the pedals off the wheelchair so I won't be uncomfortable. We sit down to have dinner, and she feeds me throughout the entire meal. And when it's over she pays the bill, pushes the wheelchair out to the car again and reverses the same routine.

And when it's over—finished—with real warmth she'll say, "Honey, thank you for taking me out to dinner." I never quite know how to answer.[9]

Now that lady is a winner who can influence practically anybody. Even while her husband was dying, she kept him *really* living by her loving. Risky? Yes. Difficult? Absolutely. But those are the challenges real winners love to take.

The winners circle is drawn with the ink of love. Get in it and be the winner God created you to be, for you really are not living unless you are loving.

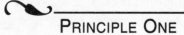

PRINCIPLE ONE
Love: Say it and show it every day.

Joy
to the World

Something we all do is such good medicine that it can relieve stress, cure headaches, fight infections, and even alleviate hypertension.

You can't do much about the length of your life, but you can do a lot about its depth and width.

Engaging in this activity produces well-documented physical benefits similar to those obtained through vigorous physical exercise.

Muscles in the abdomen, chest, shoulders, and elsewhere contract, while the heart rate and blood pressure increase. In one burst of this activity, the pulse can double from 60 to 120, while systolic blood pressure can shoot from a normal 120 to 200. Once this activity ceases, heartbeat and blood pressure also dip below normal—a sign of reduced stress.

And what is this remarkable activity? Believe it or not, it's *laughing.*[1]

Joy and Happiness: Not Siamese Twins

Laughter is good for you and laughter brings health—a fact that was known by wise King Solomon: "A merry heart does good, like medicine" (Prov. 17:22). Of course, we don't always feel like laughing. Normally we laugh because something makes us happy; when we're not happy, we usually don't laugh. But we can always enjoy a delight, a gladness of heart, a rapture in the soul that goes far beyond happiness. It is called *joy*. A tremendous difference exists between joy and happiness. We cannot be happy without being joyful, but we can be joyful without being happy. Consider a few contrasts:

- Happiness is external; joy is internal.
- Happiness depends on outward circumstances; joy depends on inward character.
- Happiness depends on what happens to us; joy depends on who lives within us.
- Happiness is based on chance; joy is based on choice.

The word *happiness* comes from the old English word *happ*, which literally means "chance." It corresponds to the Latin *fortuna*, which means "luck." These words suggest that if things happen the way we want them to happen, then we are happy. But if they don't happen the way we want, we are unhappy. Happiness is temporary and fickle; joy is permanent and settled.

God and Joy Are Three-Letter Words

Many people think God is some type of cosmic killjoy who frowns at smiles, cringes at laughter, and hates anything that smacks of joy and delight. Yet, as C. S. Lewis noted, "Joy is the serious business of heaven."

Do you know why Jesus said all that He said and why He taught all that He taught? He explained His reasons in John 15:11: "I have spoken these things to you so that My joy may be in you and your joy may be complete." The person universally accepted as the greatest teacher who ever lived said that He taught to bring joy to life.

It might surprise some to learn that the Bible uses the words *joy* and *joyful* some 250 times. The word *rejoice* appears 200 times. So the Bible instructs us to be joyful and rejoice more than 450 times.

It might seem odd that God tells us to experience joy, but that fact illustrates the difference between joy and happiness. It is true that joy sometimes just happens when good things unfold for us. No doubt we feel joy when, as the song from the musical *Oklahoma* declares, "Everything's going my way." But it is important to note that *joy is also a choice.*

The Choice Is Yours

One must understand a secret to joy before joy can be found and felt. The secret is this: Joy is more than an emotion; it's also an attitude. Emotions cannot be chosen—no one can tell you to feel happy if you are not. But you can choose to be joyful regardless of your circumstances.

"It's the economy, stupid," became the mantra that propelled Bill Clinton into the presidency of the United States. Yet too many people find out too late that money cannot buy happiness, much less joy. It has been wisely said that the poor are better off than the rich because the poor still think that money will buy happiness; the rich know better.[2]

I am reminded of a judge who spoke to a defendant who had pled guilty to robbery. "I notice that in addition to stealing money," the judge said, "you also took rings, watches, diamonds, and pearls."

"Yes, sir," the defendant replied. "I was always taught that money alone doesn't bring happiness!"

Trying to find joy in material things is like drinking saltwater: the more you drink, the thirstier you get.

A well-dressed restaurant customer was staring sullenly into his drink. The waitress, trying to be kind, asked if something was wrong.

"Well, two months ago, my grandfather died and left me $185,000 in oil wells."

"That doesn't sound like something to get upset about," the waitress replied.

"Yeah," said the young man, "but last month my uncle passed away and left me $100,000 in stocks."

"So why are you sitting there so unhappy?"

"Because this month, so far, nobody's left me a cent!"

Over two millennia ago the poet Horace wrote these words:

Happy is the man and happy is he alone,
He who can call today his own.
He who is secure within can say,
"Tomorrow do thy worst, for I have lived today."

Today is really all we have, and we can choose to be joyful today. We get to ride on the merry-go-round of life only once. So why not choose to enjoy the ride? The benefits are many.

The Power of Joy

Joy gives us strength for living. It allows us to walk in the sunshine even when the rain pours down. It gives us wings to fly when most of the world is walking. It gives us strength to persevere even under the worst circumstances. It is indeed far better to see a silver lining in every dark cloud than to see a dark lining in every silver cloud.

Furthermore, joy "baits the hook" with the one thing people want most in this world—a sense of happiness that endures with the times and doesn't evaporate with troubles. Even his political foes agreed that Ronald Reagan was one of the most well-liked presidents in our history. Why? Because of his sunny disposition. He radiated an infectious joy.[3]

Human beings spend most of their waking hours seeking something to fill the emptiness in their souls. That something is joy, and if you can offer someone joy, you will be a winner and an influencer far beyond your wildest dreams. Someone has observed that "joy is a winsome magnet that draws people in because it is the one thing they do not have."

Give the World a Smile

Dale Carnegie said that the expression you wear on your face is far more important than the clothes you wear on your back. The business guru Charles Schwab once told him that Schwab's smile had been worth a million dollars.

Carnegie tells how a New York City department store—recognizing the pressures its salesclerks felt during the Christmas rush—presented its customers with the following philosophy:

It costs nothing but creates much.

It enriches those who receive, without impoverishing those who give.

It happens in a flash and the memory of it lasts forever.

None are so rich they can get along without it, and none so poor but are richer for its benefits.

It creates happiness in the home, fosters goodwill in a business, and is the countersign of friends.

It is rest to the weary, daylight to the discouraged, sunshine to the sad, and Nature's best antidote for trouble.

Yet it cannot be bought, begged, borrowed, nor stolen, for it is something that is no earthly good to anybody until it is given away.

And if in the last-minute rush of Christmas buying some of our salespeople should be too tired to give you a smile, may we ask you to leave one of yours?

For nobody needs a smile so much as those who have none left to give![4]

When I speak of smiling, I do not mean a forced smile that shows a cynical spirit. I mean a smile that naturally reveals a heart filled with joy. Joy is difficult, if not impossible, to conceal.

Some prospectors out in California once discovered a rich vein of gold; the strike would make them all instant millionaires. They had but one problem: they had not legally staked their claim.

So they made a solemn vow to one another that they would not tell a soul about the discovery until they had completed the legal work and bought all of the supplies and tools needed to begin their digging. They went into town and divided their duties—some going to get food, others to get tools, and others to file the claim. But as they left, they noticed practically half the town was following them. At first each felt fury, believing one of them had betrayed the others. But when they asked how their discovery had leaked out, one of the townspeople replied, "It was the look of joy on your faces. We don't ever see that around here—and we knew it must be gold!" Joy and excitement so filled these men that their faces betrayed what was in their hearts.

The Journey to Joy

Think of life as a journey you can either endure or enjoy. Since you make the journey only once, you may as well enjoy the ride. Consider some practical steps that will enable you to live "on the sunny side of life."

Be a grateful person rather than a grumbling person. Gratitude is often the missing link in the chain that binds joy to the grind of everyday living. Grumbling and complaining not only take your focus off the positives; they drain the energy of joy from the battery of your heart. Stop and take notice of the little things in life for which you can feel grateful.

A man was sitting on a train, looking out the window as his railcar traveled through the countryside. Whenever the train passed open fields, he would say, "Wonderful." As it chugged through woods, the man would again say,

"Wonderful." Everything he saw—cows grazing in a pasture, birds sitting on fences, or just ordinary buildings—would evoke an amazed look and an exclamation of "Wonderful."

Another man watched him for awhile and then said, "Sir, why is everything so wonderful to you? I don't see the big deal." The man replied, "I am sure you haven't understood. You see, I have been blind since birth, but I have just had an operation and now I can see—and to me, *everything* is wonderful!"

Be satisfied with what you do have; don't sour about what you don't have. Remember two words: *greed* and *envy*. These are guaranteed joy killers. A wise person knows that more is not necessarily better, and that others are not necessarily better off. Even if the grass *is* greener on the other side, that just means it grows faster and is more difficult to cut.

A wealthy businessman felt disturbed to find a fisherman sitting lazily beside his boat. "Why aren't you out there fishing?" he asked.

"Because I've caught enough fish for today," the man replied.

"Why don't you catch more fish than you need?" The rich man asked.

"What would I do with them?"

The rich man said impatiently, "You could earn more money and buy a better boat so you could go deeper and catch more fish. You could purchase nylon nets, catch even more fish, and make more money. Soon you would have a fleet of boats and be rich like me."

"Then what would I do?" asked the fisherman.

"You could sit down and enjoy life," the rich man smugly replied.

The fisherman looked peacefully across the water, smiled, and said, "What do you think I'm doing *now?*"

That fisherman had learned the secret of enjoying life.

Invest your life in others and in something bigger than yourself. The greatest secret of personal joy—and perhaps the one principle that will practically guarantee it—is this: *Give joy to others, and you will get it for yourself.*

Helen Keller once wrote in her journal, "Many persons have a wrong idea of what constitutes happiness [and joy]. It is not attained through self-gratification but through fidelity to a worthy purpose."

Look around, and you will find that the most joyful people are those who invest their time and energy in others. The unhappiest people are those who wait around, wondering how someone is going to make them happy. Someone once asked Karl Menninger, the great psychiatrist, how a lonely and unhappy person should deal with the unhappiness. "Lock the door behind you, go across the street, find someone who is hurting, and help him or her," he replied.

Establish a personal relationship with God. This is the final step to experience joy that will stick and last a lifetime. The Bible says that in God's "presence is fullness of joy; at Your right hand are pleasures forevermore" (Ps. 16:11). God made you for Himself, and it is only when you find His purpose for your life that you will also find His peace and His joy in your life.

If you were to take a fish out of the ocean and place it on the beach, you would watch its scales dry up as it gasped for breath. Is that fish full of joy? Absolutely not. How would you give that fish joy?

If you covered it with a mountain of cash, would that make the fish joyful? No. Would a beach chair, some Ray-Bans, a good book, and some iced tea restore its joy? Of course not. Suppose you bought it a new wardrobe of double-breasted fins and people-skin shoes. Would that satisfy it? Obviously not.

Only one thing will restore joy to this fish: putting it back in the water. That fish can never have joy on the beach because it wasn't made for the beach; it was made for the ocean. In the same way, we were made for fellowship with God, and we will be like a fish out of water—never knowing the true source of real, everlasting joy—until we find it in Him.[5]

Don't Miss Out

Life is too short to miss out on the joy of knowing God, serving others, and delighting in becoming a blessing to others. Make the decision now to go through life with a smile on your face, a smile that radiates from joy in your heart. Don't be like the man described in the following ditty:

There was a very cautious man
Who never laughed or played;
He never risked, he never tried,
He never sang or prayed.
And when one day he passed away
His insurance was denied,
For since he never really lived
They claimed he never died!

PRINCIPLE TWO

Joy: By your words, actions, and looks,
brighten someone's day today.

three

How to Keep Your Head While Others Are Losing Theirs

> *First keep the peace within yourself, then you can also bring peace to others.*
>
> THOMAS
> À KEMPIS, 1420

In a recent interview, Barbara Walters asked highly accomplished actor Richard Dreyfuss a probing question: "If you could have one wish, what would you wish for?" Without hesitating, Dreyfuss replied, "Every time I have a birthday, every time I blow out candles, every time I see a shooting star, I wish the same thing—I wish for inner security."

In other words, Dreyfuss wished for peace. Most people long for *personal* peace.

What do men want most in their homes? A survey taken a few years ago revealed a shocking answer to what men care most about and hope their wives understand. Men did not want expensive furniture, well-equipped garages, or a private study. What they wanted most was tranquility at home.[1]

In other words, they wanted peace.

While in Jerusalem, I once took a taxi down to the Old City. The cab driver, a young Jewish man named Asi, eagerly responded to my questions about spiritual matters. "What do you believe about the Messiah?" I asked.

"I believe the most important thing that can ever happen to Israel is for Messiah to come," he replied.

"Why do you believe that?"

"Because He will bring peace!" he said forcefully.

People long for *political* peace.

We need peace, not just between next-door neighbors but between nations as well. In a total of 3,530 years of recorded civilization, only 286 years have been spent without war raging some place on the globe. Yet during that same period, eight thousand peace treaties have been signed.[2] One wag said, "Peace is the brief, glorious moment in history when everybody stands around reloading."

Do you realize that all of the peace monuments built in Washington, D.C., were erected after a war? I am convinced that the primary cause of our difficulty in maintaining external peace is our lack of internal peace.

Recently, I saw a large plaque near the United Nations building in New York, bearing Isaiah 2:4—"They shall beat their swords into plowshares, and their spears into pruning hooks; nation shall not lift up sword against nation, neither shall they learn war anymore." Unfortunately, this is a prophecy yet to be fulfilled.

Even though part of the charter of the U.N. reads, "Our purpose is to maintain international peace and security and to that end: to take effective, collective measures for the prevention and removal of threats to the peace," I am convinced that the noble effort is doomed without peace of another sort. The kind of peace I want to address is more than the absence of war; it is the presence of an inward, personal peace that cannot be blown about by the winds of current events, nor does it depend on the ever-changing circumstances of life.

Messed Up and Stressed Out

We live in the most technologically advanced time in history. I feel grateful for the many amenities that make my life so much easier. As I write, I am serving as the president of the Southern Baptist Convention, the largest evangelical Christian denomination in the world. The position could easily be a full-time job. I would be dead in the water were it not for cell phones, PalmPilots, fax machines, E-mail, laptop computers, the Internet, laser printers, photocopy machines, jet planes, and automobiles equipped with satellite navigational systems (to name a few).

Yet these same technological marvels create problems of their own. A recent *USA Today* article detailed how high-tech gadgets boost not only productivity but stress. It described how therapist Ofér Zur staged a conference called "Speed.com: The Search for Meaning in the New Millennium" in the heart of stressed-out Silicon Valley. Zur could see the drawn faces, worried looks, and preoccupied demeanors in his audience. He said that "his personal alarm sounded when patients started bringing cell phones and laptops to his practice—and using them during the session!"

Zur further observed, "We've become obsessed with speed. We end up with lots of plans that we can't execute and a full schedule that can't be followed. The paradox of our timesaving tech gadgets is that we've wound up with no free time."[3]

One stressed-out secretary told her boss, "When this rush is over, I'm going to have a nervous breakdown. I earned it. I deserve it. And nobody's going to take it from me!"

Can you relate to this woman? Frankly, at this stage of my life I am so busy that I don't have the time to have a nervous breakdown—and if I did, I would be too busy to enjoy it!

The problem of speed has no doubt added to the mess of stress. Without question, our warp-speed pace is taking a heavy toll. In short, *increasing our pace has decreased our peace.* Not long ago we marked the passage of time in seasons. But seasons begat monthly calendars, which begat day planners, which begat one-minute managers, which begat hand-held personal organizers, and so on and so on.

One can see cyberstress and hyperstress everywhere. Go to the grocery store and see how much small talk you get from the cashier, whose speed and efficiency is being tracked by computer even as she electronically scans your groceries, calls out your total, and digitally sweeps you out the door. Try engaging telephone solicitors or directory-assistance operators in any meaningful dialogue and you won't succeed; they work under precise, by-the-minute efficiency guidelines. The result of this fast-paced, time-warped approach? Increasing impatience, intolerance, and a lack of civility.[4]

The workplace is no doubt a major incubator where stress is fed, nurtured, and kept warm. Lou Harris & Associates recently conducted a national study of the changing workforce for the Families and Work Institute. This five-year study sought in-depth information from nearly three thousand salaried and hourly employees. When asked, "How tough are today's jobs?" and other questions, 88 percent of the respondents said they work "very hard"; 68 percent said they work "very fast"; 60 percent said they still don't get work done; 71 percent feel "used up." The research concluded that "workers are more frazzled, insecure, and torn between work and family than they were in 1977."[5]

Not even ministers are immune, as I can personally attest. In fact, they may be most in need of the peace they preach in their pulpits every week. In a recent *Los Angeles Times* article, psychologist Richard Blackmon claimed that "pastors are the single most occupationally frustrated group in America." About 75 percent of pastors go through a period of stress so great that they consider quitting the ministry; 35 to 40 percent actually resign. Incidents of mental breakdown are so high that insurance companies charge about 4 percent extra to cover church staff members, compared to employees in other professions.[6]

H. B. London, assistant to the president of Focus on the Family, cites a Fuller Institute of Church Growth study that found 90 percent of pastors work more than forty-six hours a week; 90 percent feel that they have inadequate training to cope with ministry demands; 50 percent feel unable to meet the needs of the job; 75 percent report a significant stress-related crisis at least once in their ministry; 80 percent believe that pastoral ministry has a negative affect on their families; and 33 percent say that being in the ministry is downright hazardous to their families.[7]

No one is immune to stress, frustration, and the feeling that we are on the autobahn of life—and the only two travelers on this superhighway are the quick and the dead. The very word *stress* comes from the Latin word *strictus,* which means "to be drawn tight," with the idea of feeling distress. What is all this but the absence of peace? In this maelstrom of daily living, the stock value of peace increases every moment.

Peace Is an Inside Job

The Bible speaks a great deal about peace, describing three kinds of peace in particular. First, there is peace with others. "If possible, on your part, live at peace with everyone," said the apostle Paul in Romans 12:18. This is *external* peace, necessary for human relationships to flourish, whether in neighborhoods or nations.

Second, there is peace with yourself. The Scripture speaks of letting the "peace of the Messiah . . . control your hearts" (Col. 3:15). This is *internal* peace—the inner tranquility that escapes most people today.

Finally, the Bible speaks of peace with God; this is *eternal* peace (see Rom. 5:1). This is the peace that comes from knowing that one has a right relationship with the sovereign God of this universe.

As I write, violence has exploded once more in the Middle East. In the West Bank and the Gaza Strip, clashes between Israelis and Palestinians have left more than ninety dead. Observers and pundits both claim repeatedly that "the peace process is dead."

Maybe so; maybe not. But one thing is true: *Peace is a process.* Peace is not a goal to be achieved but a process in which one type of peace leads to another. You cannot be

at true peace with others until you are at peace with yourself. But you can never be totally and truly at peace with
yourself unless you are at peace with God, for all true
peace flows from the only One who can give peace.

People are looking for peace today in every place but
the right place. Why? Because they do not understand this
principle. Some try to find peace in pills or pleasure or
possessions but discover too late that these things offer
only a synthetic, counterfeit peace that always wears off
and wears out.

In 1987, former Minnesota Twins superstar Kirby
Puckett saw a childhood dream come true in leading his
team to the championship of the World Series. Greg
Gagne, the Twins shortstop, was asked to describe the
scene in the clubhouse after their win. He recounted the
hugging, the shouting, the laughing, the obligatory dous-
ing of champagne over the players' heads, and the presen-
tation of the trophy. But the memory that would stick with
him forever, he said, occurred when he noticed the normally ebullient Puckett sitting silently on a stool away from
everyone, only ten minutes into the celebration. Gagne
wove his way through the media, players, and coaches, sat
down beside Puckett and asked him to describe his
thoughts. With a deep sadness in his eyes, Puckett said, "If
this is all there is to it, life is pretty empty."[8]

You may be able to relate to that millionaire ballplayer.
You may have a great job, an excellent salary, a fine house,
a wonderful family, good health, and maybe even a low
handicap—*but no real personal peace.* You lack the kind of
inward peace that knows that even though life often feels
like a runaway roller coaster, there is a Hand on the
throttle that keeps everything under control.

The Hebrew term for this kind of peace is *shalom*. This is the peace spoken of in Isaiah 26:3: "You will keep him in perfect peace, whose mind is stayed on You, because he trusts in You."

Apart from God, enduring peace will always remain a pipe dream, a philosophical fantasy, a tantalizing fish always just beyond any bait or hook.

A Peace Treaty with the Soul

Let me let you in on a little secret. Peace is not the absence of problems but the presence of God in the midst of your problems. The reason most people never find peace is because they are looking for it. No one ever finds peace by looking for peace. Why not? Because peace is not something you find; it finds you when you focus on the God who gives peace.

So many marriages go awry because men and women think an imperfect person can give them the perfect peace for which they are searching. Have you heard the story of a woman at a cocktail party trying her best to look happy? Someone noticed a gargantuan sparkling rock on her finger and exclaimed, "Wow! What a beautiful diamond!"

"Yes," she said, "it's a Callahan diamond."

"I wish I had one!" the onlooker replied.

"No, you don't," the woman tartly responded.

"Why not?"

"Because it comes with the Callahan curse."

"The Callahan curse—what's that?"

With a deep sigh and a forlorn look, she said, "Mr. Callahan!"

Perfect peace can come only from a perfect peace-giver; and the only One who meets that qualification is God!

People are looking not only for peace but also for those who manifest that peace in their lives. The great leaders who inspire great followings project a sense of serenity and peace even when everything around them is falling apart. The peers of Abraham Lincoln said that even in the darkest days of the Civil War, when the North endured defeat after defeat, the president never displayed a sense of panic in his heart or on his face. Instead, he manifested a peace born of an unshakable confidence in a provident God and a just cause.

Lincoln knew what a lot of stressed-out worrywarts need to learn: *Peace is a matter of focus.* A tremendous passage of Scripture states, "You will keep him in perfect peace, whose mind is stayed on You" (Isa. 26:3). Focusing on circumstances will cause constant anxiety, for circumstances constantly change and often spin beyond our control. But God never changes and nothing spins beyond His control.

Peace and worry are mutually exclusive. The word *worry* comes from the old German term *wurgen,* which literally means "to struggle" or "to choke." Worry throttles our confidence, chokes our perspective, and suffocates our spirit. Worry robs us of the peace that comes from knowing the God who can handle anything and for whom all things are possible.

What is worry, and what does it do?

First, worry is *distrust in the wisdom of God.* Every time you worry, you are really saying, "God, I don't believe You can handle this. I don't believe You can be trusted in this matter. I guess I'm going to have to carry this burden all by myself."

Second, worry is a *denial of the Word of God*. When you worry, you are really saying that God does not keep His promises. You think He lies or exaggerates when He says things such as the promise of Romans 8:28: "All things work together for the good of those who love God"?

I wish we could all take a cue from a man who was a tremendous worrier. He not only worried; he worried others with his worry. He couldn't sleep because he worried so much; all he would do was pace the floor. One day he came out of his house a totally different person. He was whistling, happy, and singing at the top of his lungs. His next-door neighbor saw him and asked, "What in the world has happened to you?"

"Oh," he replied, "I don't have a worry in this world, and I am so happy."

"And how did you get rid of your worries?" the neighbor wondered.

"Well, I have hired a professional worrier," he answered. "He does all of my worrying for me."

"That's just wonderful. How much does this professional worrier cost?"

"He costs a thousand dollars a day."

"A thousand dollars a day? You don't have that kind of money. How are you going to pay him?"

"Oh, that's his worry," answered the man.

There is Someone to whom you can give *all* of your problems so that you can enjoy peace even in the most difficult times. As the Bible says, "[Cast] all your care upon Him, because He cares about you" (1 Pet. 5:7).

In the Eye of the Storm

One of the most powerful natural forces known to man is a hurricane. With winds of up to 155 miles per hour, rain up to five inches per hour, and the ability to create waves ten stories high and wave surges up to twenty-five feet in diameter, hurricanes can level whole cities in minutes.

Two components of a hurricane are especially interesting. One is the eye of a hurricane—the relatively calm center of circulation in which sinking air inhibits cloud and thunderstorm development. Immediately surrounding the eye is the eyewall, which features rising air and powerful rain clouds. In sharp contrast to the calm eye, the eyewall houses the most powerful element of the hurricane, including the strongest winds and the heaviest rains.

If you could hover above this incredibly powerful force of nature, you would see the strongest part of a hurricane occurring near its center, while at its center would be relative calm, with no thunderstorms and little or no cloud cover.

In the presidential election of 2000, our nation weathered a political storm, the likes of which I had never seen. The election hinged on the state of Florida and its twenty-five electoral votes. All around blew the winds of recounts and the rains of lawsuits and countersuits. We were buffeted about by the hurricane of division, uncertainty, and bitterness, perhaps not seen in this nation since the end of the Civil War.

In the middle of all this turmoil, I was intrigued by a comment made by Jeb Bush, brother of George W. Bush. When asked by a reporter if his brother was on pins and needles, Jeb Bush replied, "No, he is actually at total peace." I then learned that George W. Bush was staying at his ranch, watching no television, just reading his Bible as he does each morning, spending time with his family, and, in so many words, trusting God for the outcome. That is what I call being in the eye of the storm.

Oceanographers tell us that the worst ocean storm never goes more than twenty-five feet deep beneath the surface. In other words, gales can rip the ocean, causing tidal waves one hundred feet high. But just twenty-five feet below the surface, the water is as calm as a pond on a sunny day in June.

The only place you will ever find peace in the midst of the storm is down deep in a walk with God. The peace found in God, through the Holy Scriptures and prayer, cannot be found, bought, or manufactured anywhere else.

The Korean Christians have a saying that emerged when they were being persecuted because of their faith in Christ. "We are just like nails," they say. "The harder you hit us, the deeper you drive us; and the deeper you drive us, the more peaceful it becomes."

Part of God's purpose in allowing the storms to blow is to do just that—to drive us deeper. Someone once said, "God takes life's broken pieces and gives us unbroken peace." Horatio Spafford made that discovery in his own experience.

Spafford was born in 1828. He became a real estate baron and an extremely wealthy man, yet he depended upon God for personal peace through a strong relationship with Christ. He lived in Chicago, and during the great Chicago fire, he lost his business and his only son. It seemed as though a canopy of dark clouds covered his life.

His wife felt tremendous stress, so he put her and their four daughters on a ship to England, which was her home country. He told them he would join them two weeks later.

In sight of land, a terrible storm hit, and all four of Spafford's daughters drowned. Only his wife survived. She sent a telegram to him with these two words: "Saved alone."

With the heaviest of hearts, Horatio Spafford got on a ship, made his way across the Atlantic to England, met his wife, and with her reboarded the ship to come back. On the return voyage he asked the captain to show him the exact spot where the other ship went down. When they reached the spot, Spafford went out on deck and wrote the following words:

> When peace like a river attendeth my way,
>> When sorrows like sea billows roll;
> Whatever my lot, Thou has taught me to say,
>> It is well, it is well with my soul.[9]

How do we explain such peace in the middle of such a devastating storm? It is a matter of *focus* and *faith*. The only way we can keep our heads while others are losing theirs is to focus on an all-powerful God who remains in control and in charge and does all things well.

I leave you with this thought: *If there is within you the One who reigns above you, you will not succumb to that which is around you.*

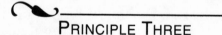

Principle Three

*For peace, stay cool on the inside when it's hot
on the outside by trusting God
to handle every problem, big or small.*

Winners Never Quit and Quitters Never Win

A first grade teacher and her class of thirty-two pupils had watched it rain all day. Finally, the last bell rang. It was time to go home. The teacher began putting galoshes on all thirty-two of her first-graders.

> *Feather by feather the goose is plucked.*
> JOHN RAY

She came to the last little girl and felt great excitement that her dirty task was almost finished. Yet the galoshes seemed unusually tight. The teacher struggled, she strained, she pulled, she tugged, she grunted, she groaned—and finally got the galoshes on. Just as she finished snapping them into place, the little girl said, "You know what, teacher? These aren't my galoshes."

The teacher couldn't believe it. With a tremendous sigh she struggled, she strained, she pulled, she tugged, she grunted, she groaned, until glistening with sweat she finally yanked the galoshes off the little girl's feet. At the moment she snapped them off, the little girl looked up at her and said sweetly, "They're my sister's, and she lets me wear them."

I will be the first to admit that I need patience. I tell the Lord all the time, "I want patience, and I want it right now!" Do you have a problem with patience?

I need to be more like the little boy in a department store. He was at the end of an escalator, watching the railing as it went around. A salesman came by and asked him, "Son, are you lost?"

"No," said the little boy, "I'm just waiting for my chewing gum to come back."

Very little in life has ever been accomplished without the virtue of patience (that's what the Bible calls "long-suffering"). What is long-suffering? *Long-suffering is the willingness to exercise patience, perseverance, and persistence in the pursuit of worthy goals.*

The Greek word for "long-suffering" is *makrothymîa* from a combination of two Greek words—the word *makro,* which means "long or slow," and the word *thymîa,* which means "anger." Their combination literally means to be long-tempered. Patience is the ability to be slow to anger, rather than quick to anger.

Life is not a hundred-yard dash; it is a marathon. To reach the finish line victoriously, you need to remember three things every morning as you lace up those shoes and begin the next stage of the race.

Winners Exercise Patience with Difficult People

Only hermits and hobos can avoid dealing with difficult people. Not even monks in monasteries are exempt from this task.

One man decided to join a monastery because he was tired of dealing with difficult people. He rose to become the head monk and felt deliriously happy until an extremely negative man joined the monastery.

The head monk told the man of the rule everybody had to keep: Say only two words every year. At the end of the first year the man came in to see the head monk who asked him, "What are your two words?"

"Bed hard," the man replied.

At the end of the second year the man once again trudged into the head monk's office and with a glare said, "Room cold."

At the end of the third year, the man said with lips trembling, "Food terrible."

Finally, at the end of the fourth year the man walked in and screamed, "I quit!" The head monk shot back with, "Great! All you've done since you've been here is complain, complain, complain!"

One can learn much from an ordinary farmer about patience. A farmer plants, weeds, waters, and cultivates. Every day he does two things: watch and wait. He knows that the harvest will come if he will just be patient. He knows that he cannot hurry the harvest. For it will come in due time.

What is true of plants is also true of people. Many of us have seen the bumper sticker that states: "Please be patient with me; God is not finished with me yet." What is true of us is also true of others. Anyone can explode when people mess up, foul up, and blow it. It takes a special person to respond with grace and calmness when the heat is on because somebody else started the fire.

Someone has said that "patience is the ability to idle your motor when you feel like stripping your gears." Of course, patience is not passivity. It is not indifference. It is not a fatalistic attitude toward life that sits back, twiddles its thumbs, and says, "Whatever will be, will be."

Patience does not mean that you never get angry because anger is not always wrong. Sometimes a lack of anger is wrong. Patience means you are slow to anger and quick to get rid of it. Too often we are just the opposite: We are quick to be angry and slow to get rid of it—and that is when the acid of anger turns into the burden of bitterness. Then we either hold grudges or try to get even. We can even appear to be patient with others when we really are not.

Some American soldiers during the Korean War rented a house and hired a local boy to do their house-keeping and cooking. Their little Korean fellow had an unbelievably positive attitude—he was always smiling and jovial and happy. So they played one trick after another on him.

They nailed his shoes to the floor. He would just get up in the morning, pull out the nails with pliers, slip on the shoes, and keep on smiling.

They put grease on the stove handles. He would just wipe each one off and keep smiling and singing.

They balanced buckets of water over the door. When he would open the door, he would get drenched. He would simply dry off and never fuss and keep on smiling.

Finally, they became so ashamed of themselves that they called him in and said, "We want you to know that we are never going to trick you again. We really do appreciate your patience."

"You mean, no more nail shoes to floor?" he asked.

"No more."

"You mean, no more sticky on stove knobs?"

"No more."

"You mean, no more water buckets on door?"

"No more."

"OK then," he replied, "no more spit in soup."

You cannot get away from individuals who are going to try your patience. In fact, the people you love the most will try your patience the most. If you have been married more than three days, you know that to be true (but I have yet to meet a couple married for fifty years or more who have regretted staying together).

By and large, marriages fail for one basic reason: One or both parties simply quit. In any relationship, whether at home or at the office, patience can salvage partnerships that are really worth keeping. Difficulties are simply opportunities in disguise to help you cultivate the virtue of patience.

Winners Practice Perseverance with Demanding Problems

Determination is a first cousin to patience. As I look back on my own life, I can see that the really meaningful accomplishments did not come without difficulties and opposition. Along the way I always had the option to give up, give out, or give in—but only if I wanted to admit defeat.

One of my heroes is a man we hear little about, but he affects the lives of millions around the world who turn on a light or listen to recorded music. His influence lives on today because he maintained an unswerving, even steely determination to see projects through to completion.

Life magazine named him the number one man of the past millennium. He had an astounding number of inventions—1,093—and held more patents than any other person in the world, receiving at least one every year for sixty-five consecutive years. He also developed the modern research laboratory. His name: Thomas Alva Edison.

Most experts credit Edison's ability to creative genius; he credited it to hard work. "Genius," he declared, "is ninety-nine percent perspiration and one percent inspiration." I believe he succeeded in part because of a third factor: his positive attitude.

The optimistic Edison saw the best in everything. "If we did all the things we were capable of doing," he once said, "we would literally astound ourselves." After ten thousand tries, he still couldn't find the right material for the incandescent light bulb, but he didn't see the unsuccessful attempts as failures. With each attempt he gained information about what didn't work, bringing him closer to a solution. He never doubted that he would find a good one. His belief could be summarized by this statement: "Many of life's failures are people who did not realize how close they were to success when they gave up."[1]

Every time I turn on a light so I won't stumble in the dark, I am so grateful that Edison didn't quit. Just think—if it had not been for perseverance, the snail never would have made it to Noah's ark.

Problems are not meant to defeat you, depress you, or discourage you. God meant them to develop you. Problems are not tools to tear you down but tests to build you up. One mark of a successful person is the ability to see problems as opportunities rather than obstacles. The greatest lessons you will ever learn occur not when you party during the good times but when you persevere in the bad times. Indeed, that is why the bad times make the good times so good.

Have you ever read about the birth of a giraffe? The first parts to emerge are the baby's front hooves and head. Then the entire calf appears and tumbles ten feet to the ground, landing on its back. Within seconds it rolls over and stands, struggling with those gangly, untried legs. Then an amazing thing happens: The mother giraffe positions herself directly over her newborn calf and looks it over. Then she swings a long leg outward and kicks that baby, sending it sprawling. If it doesn't get up, she kicks it again. If it grows tired, she kicks it again to stimulate its efforts to stand.

Each time the baby giraffe manages to get to its feet, its mother kicks it over again. The mother's actions may seem cruel to us, but she is acting that way for a reason. She is preparing that little calf for survival. The calf must learn to get up quickly and run with the herd when danger comes or it will not survive.

When life kicks you and knocks you down, you have to get back up. At certain times in life, you must either stand or die—there will be situations that leave no other choice. During those difficult times, you will learn some of the greatest lessons in life through sheer determination and perseverance.

William Wilberforce was a member of the British Parliament and a dear friend of John Newton, the former slave who wrote the beloved hymn "Amazing Grace." Wilberforce was a tremendous Christian who crusaded in Parliament to outlaw slavery in all of the British Empire. He begged, pleaded, and introduced bills, and each time he would be laughed down, shouted down, and voted down. On his deathbed, the British Parliament finally signed the bill outlawing slavery throughout the British Empire. How long did it take? Fifty years. Thank God he didn't quit.

Don't Quit

When things go wrong, as they sometimes will,
When the road you're trudging seems all uphill,
When the funds are low and the debts are high,
And you want to smile, but you have to sigh,
When care is pressing you down a bit . . .
Rest if you must, but don't you dare quit.

When you are worried and full of doubt,
Just remember that success is failure turned
    inside out . . .
So stick to the fight when you're hardest hit,
It's when things seem worst that you mustn't quit.
          —William Murray Angus

While I cannot guarantee that perseverance will bring success, I can guarantee that if you lack perseverance—if you leave the kitchen when things heat up—you will be a failure. You are not a failure until you quit; but when you quit, you are a failure. Quitters never win and winners never quit. It is not how you start but how you finish that counts.

If you could accomplish only one thing in life, what would it be? Write it down, and for thirty days do two things: (1) Look yourself in the mirror and say, "Just for today, I am going to take one step toward achieving this goal," and (2) *take that one step.* At the end of the thirty days, you will be amazed at how much of that book you read, how much of that weight you lost, how much of that money you were able to save. And you will have seen the awesome power of determination to boot.

Winners Develop Persistence with a Definite Purpose

Why should you develop the discipline of patience, perseverance, and persistence? You ought to build stick-to-it-iveness in dealing with people or problems not just for what it allows you to do but rather *what it does for you.*

Troubles and troublemakers come into your life to force you to develop the discipline of long-suffering, and you will never reach the peak of your potential until you enroll in the school of hard knocks and learn the discipline of patience and perseverance.

Do you know why these character qualities seem so difficult to develop? *Because they involve waiting.* One of the most difficult things to do in life is wait. In a country that exists on frozen dinners, instant mashed potatoes, powdered orange drink, packaged cake mixes, instant print cameras, and freeway express lanes, it's difficult to learn how to wait.

Be honest. Wouldn't you rather do anything than wait? If the truth were known, sometimes we would rather do the wrong thing than wait.

Jell-O celebrated its one-hundredth anniversary in 1997. However, if its inventor were still alive, he probably would have taken little comfort in his product's success.

In 1897, Pearl Wait wore several hats. He was a construction worker who also dabbled in patent medicines and went door-to-door selling his remedies. In the midst of his tinkering, he came upon the idea of mixing fruit flavoring with granulated gelatin. His wife named it "Jell-O," and Wait thought he just had one more product to peddle. Unfortunately, sales were not as strong as he had hoped they would be, so in 1899 Pearl Wait sold his Jell-O rights to Orator Woodward for $450. Woodward knew the value of marketing, so within eight brief years, Wait's neighbor turned a $450 investment into a $1 million business.

Today, not a single relative of Pearl Wait receives one penny from the 1.1 million boxes of Jell-O sold every day. Why not? Because Wait just couldn't wait.[2]

There is no such thing as instant success, whether with people or problems. Whether one needs to lose ten pounds or a hundred, the weight can be shed only one pound at a time. It is not the standing on top of the mountain that is such a thrill; it is the getting there through a determined climb that makes it all worthwhile.

Though I grew up in Georgia and love my state, when it comes to baseball, I am unashamedly a New York Yankees fan. I grew up listening to Dizzy Dean and Pee Wee Reese call the Yankees game of the week every Saturday afternoon. My hero and idol was Mickey Mantle.

One of my greatest thrills in life was the time I went with my son Jonathan to see the Yankees play the Atlanta Braves at historic (and, might I say, "hallowed") Yankee Stadium. There we saw the monuments to Ruth, Gehrig, and Di Maggio. Does it get any better?

The Yankees have won four of the last six World Series and three in a row from 1998 to 2000. By all accounts, the team's recent success is due in no small part to the leadership of their manager, Joe Torre. His face was plastered all over magazines and featured in many commercials. He is revered as one of the best managers in all of baseball.

What many do not know is that it took Joe Torre 4,272 games as a player and a manager to get to the World Series—the longest wait for anyone in the history of the game. As Torre reflected on his achievements, so long in the making, he offered the following remarks:

> As a manager prior to coming to the Yankees, my win-loss record was 119 games below .500 . . . [yet] I never gave in to the idea that I was somehow a failure. . . . Baseball is such a perfect metaphor for life [because of its] 162-game schedule—the "grind" I have known for thirty-two years—is in fact much closer to the daily lives of most people. You get up every morning, do your best, make small steps forward, suffer setbacks that obscure your long-term progress, fight off hassles and absurd obstacles, and once in a blue moon, you actually achieve a cherished goal that's been the stuff of your dreams. Then, with the world's permission, you can call yourself a winner. But only you know how many small triumphs and snarls went into that big victory, how many months, years, or decades of sweat and sorrow preceded that breakthrough. That's baseball, and that's life.[3]

Joe Torre is living proof that if you quit, you neither win nor live in the truest sense of the word.

One of my dearest minister friends signs his letters with "Hang in the Battle." That is my final advice to you. Those who determine to fight until their last breath will always end up winners.

Principle Four

Just for today, in dealing with people and problems, hang in there and don't quit!

five

Try
a Little Kindness

After Confederate general Robert E.
Lee retired from the military, he was
named president of Washington
and Lee University in Lexington,
Virginia, which was originally
named Washington Academy

*Kindness is the oil
that takes the
friction out of life.*
ANONYMOUS

because of a gift from George Washington. The name was
changed in 1871 in honor of General Lee.

While Lee served as president of the university, a new
student came into his office and asked for a copy of the
school's rules and regulations. Lee looked at him and said,
"Son, we don't have any rules and regulations in print."

"You mean, this school has no rules?" the young man
asked.

"Yes, we have only one," Lee replied.

"What is it?"

"Our only rule is kindness," the former general
replied.[1]

Once in saying good-bye to his nephew, the noted
American novelist Henry James said something the boy

never forgot. Although known for his witty, impenetrable writings, James offered this clear advice: "Billy, there are three things that are important in human life. The first is to be kind; the second is to be kind; and the third is to be kind."

We live in a society in which kindness is becoming an increasingly rare commodity. Not long ago, the cover story of *USA Today* began with this observation: "A surly driver cuts into your lane. Your teenager brings home a CD with lewd, hostile lyrics. A political candidate in a TV ad morphs into a convicted murderer. A star baseball player spits at an umpire. A radio talk show jockey insults the president while he's sitting right there . . . it is impossible to ignore the growing rudeness, even harshness, of American life."[2]

We have become a society in which the milk of human kindness has curdled. An overwhelming majority of Americans—89 percent in a *U.S. News & World Report* poll—think incivility is a serious problem. More than three in four respondents said it has gotten worse in the last ten years.[3]

We live in a culture increasingly known for its coarseness rather than its kindness. When we begin to see people as numbers or inconveniences rather than as individuals, kindness goes out the window. This is precisely what humorist Robert Henry encountered one evening when he visited a large discount department store in search of a pair of binoculars.

As he walked up to the appropriate counter, he noticed he was the only customer in the store. Behind the counter stood two salespeople. One was so preoccupied talking to "Mama" on the telephone that she refused even to acknowledge Robert. At the other end of the counter, a second salesperson was unloading inventory from a box onto the shelves. Growing impatient, Robert walked down to her end of the counter and just stood there. Finally, she looked up at Robert and said, "You got a number?"

"I got a *what?*" asked Robert, trying to control his astonishment.

"You got a number? You gotta have a number."

"Lady," Robert replied, "I'm the only customer in the store! I don't need a number. Can't you see how ridiculous this is?" But she failed to see the absurdity and insisted that Robert take a number before agreeing to wait on him. By now, it was obvious to Robert that she was more interested in following procedures than in helping her customer. So he went to the number dispenser, pulled number thirty-seven, and walked back to the salesperson. With that, she promptly went to her number counter, which revealed that the last customer had been holding number thirty-four. So she screamed out, "Thirty-five! . . . Thirty-five! . . . Thirty-six! . . . thirty-six! . . . Thirty-seven!"

"I'm number thirty-seven," said Robert.

"May I help you?" she asked without cracking a smile.

"No," replied Robert, and he turned around and walked out.[4]

I surfed the Internet recently looking for the word *kindness* and discovered a nonprofit organization called "The Kindness Society." Note their stated purpose: "We are striving to spread kindness by following a simple rule: Do not think, speak, or act unkindly toward others."

Everybody can relate to kindness and everyone can respond with kindness. Mark Twain once said, "Kindness is a language which the deaf can hear, and the blind can read."

Still, being kind can be risky and even downright difficult. It is risky because it can be misunderstood. We have all endured those experiences where we tried to be kind, but our efforts were taken the wrong way or we unwittingly said the wrong thing.

A woman carried her newborn onto a bus and the driver said, "That's the ugliest baby I've ever seen!" The lady slammed her money into the fare box and stomped back to a seat at the rear of the bus. The man next to her asked her what was wrong and she said, "The bus driver was very rude to me!"

"That's outrageous," he replied. "He shouldn't be insulting the passengers."

"I think I'll go up there and give him a piece of my mind," said the lady.

"Good idea," answered the man. "And while you're up there, I'll hold your monkey for you."

Sometimes kindness is the last thing on your mind, and it is a chore to give even a crumb of kindness. A young man went to work in the produce section of a supermarket. It was his first day on the job and a lady approached him, requesting to buy half of a head of lettuce. He tried to dissuade her, but she persisted. Finally he said, "I'll have to go back and talk to the manager."

He walked to the rear of the store to talk to the manager, not realizing the woman had followed him. When he reached the manager, he said, "There's some stupid old lady out here who wants to buy half a head of lettuce. What should I tell her?"

Noting the horrified look on the face of the manager, the boy turned around, saw the woman, and quickly said, "And this nice lady wants to buy the other half. Is that all right?" Considerably relieved, the manager said, "That would be fine."

Later in the day, the manager congratulated the boy on his quick thinking. He then asked him, "Where are you from, son?"

"I'm from Toronto, Canada, the home of beautiful hockey players and ugly women," the boy replied.

The manager glared at him and said, "My wife is from Toronto."

"Oh," said the young man. "What team did she play for?"

It is hard to go wrong with kindness. Sometimes when we pay people a compliment, they will say, "You're too kind." In fact, what they really mean is, "Play it again, Sam!" We all hunger to be treated with courtesy and kindness.

The King of Kindness

Jesus Christ would probably be universally acclaimed as the kindest person who ever lived. He, too, came into an unkind world, a dog-eat-dog, every-man-for-himself culture. No organizations of mercy, mental institutions, hospitals, or orphanages existed then. Yet when Jesus came, He poured the milk of human kindness into every bowl of human suffering. No one ever accused Him of being unkind, even His most bitter enemies.

He teaches us that we should be kind not only to those who don't deserve our kindness but also to those who are unthankful and unappreciative of our kindness. Even in His life, acts of kindness were misunderstood. His greatest act of kindness—His death on the cross—was misunderstood and even reviled by much of the world. But He teaches us a real lesson about kindness: Kindness costs. Kindness costs a great deal but cannot be bought at any price.

Let the Light of Kindness Shine in Your Life

Sometimes we get the idea that leaders must be tough, hard, and practically stoic in the way they relate to others, so much so that kindness is viewed as a weakness or vulnerability for them. I strongly disagree. I believe that kindness signals tremendous inner strength that others not only appreciate but respect.

Tenderness and kindness can motivate people to do things that toughness never can. Aesop wrote a fable in which the wind and the sun argued over who was the stronger. "Do you see that old man down there?" asked the wind. "I can make him take his coat off quicker than you can."

The sun agreed to duck behind a cloud while the wind blew up a storm. The harder the wind blew, however, the more firmly the old man wrapped his coat around him.

Eventually, the wind gave up and the sun reappeared, smiling kindly upon that old man. Before long, the old man mopped his brow, pulled off his coat, and strolled on his way. The sun knew the secret: Warmth, friendliness, and a gentle touch are always stronger than force and fury.

One of the greatest marks of leadership—and one of the keys to building lasting relationships—is kindness. It is nice to be important, but it is more important to be nice.

Once while Abraham Lincoln was dining in the White House, one of his guests proved to be lacking in good manners. He blew on his coffee, poured the coffee into his saucer, and drank out of the saucer.

As you might imagine, some of the refined ladies seated near him were aghast. For a moment the room was filled with an embarrassing silence. Then Abraham Lincoln took his coffee, poured it into the saucer, and for the rest of the evening he also drank out of the saucer. Everyone else in the room followed suit. One small act of kindness had saved a man from unbelievable embarrassment. That simple yet thoughtful gesture by one of our greatest presidents reminds me of a quote by William Wordsworth: "That best portion of a good man's life; his little, nameless unremembered acts of kindness and love."

Probably you never have heard of Stephen Grellett, a French-born Quaker who died in New Jersey in 1855. He would remain unknown to the world today except for a few lines that will be remembered forever. "I shall pass through this world but once," he said. "Any good that I can do, or any kindness that I can show to any human being, let me do it now and not defer it. For I shall not pass this way again."

Kindness: Don't Leave Home without It

Every day has at least one thing in common with the next: the opportunity to show kindness. Let someone move in front of you in the flow of traffic. Open a door for a lady. Help people with their overhead luggage. Opportunities missed are not only gone, but they can be extremely embarrassing.

My youngest son attends a Christian academy. The drive to his school includes a two-lane road that eventually turns into a one-lane road. Every morning, cars in the left lane have to allow cars in the right lane to merge.

Sometimes it can seem as exciting and as cutthroat as the Daytona 500.

One morning I was in the right lane, attempting to merge into the left lane. A van to my left had plenty of room in front, so I sped up to get into the free space, but the van sped up, cutting me off. This occurred so close to the end of the lane that I had to slam on my brakes until the van passed. I was not a happy camper.

I followed this van only to see the driver turn into the same school. Then I noticed the religious symbols and bumper stickers on the back of the vehicle. I thanked God I was not an unbeliever just looking for another reason to criticize hypocritical Christians.

I hope that driver regretted her action and was moved to shame for her selfishness and inconsideration. I have long forgotten what she looked like or even the kind of van she drove. But I wish I could send her this poem:

> I have wept in the night
> For the shortness of sight,
> That to somebody's need made me blind:
> But I never have yet felt a twinge of regret,
> For being a little too kind.[5]

Let the Music of Kindness Sound through Your Lips

Everyone in the world has a "kindness kit" that you carry everywhere with you. It lives in your mouth and is called the tongue.

Never underestimate the power of just one kind word. A Japanese proverb says, "One kind word can warm three winter months."

Jim Elliot, a famous missionary who gave his life to spread the gospel in the jungles of South America, wrote the following words in his journal:

I spoke,
Words fell
Aimlessly on ears;
Later one said,
"Your word—it helped that day."
I turned wondering,
Forgot I said that word;
Let me speak
Those words often;
Helpful words
That I forget.[6]

Anyone can *react* with kindness to acts of kindness. The real challenge is to *respond* with kindness to those who lack it. It is one thing to be kind to those who like us and treat us well; it's another thing to be kind to those who don't. And it is so important, as much as we can, to be kind not only with deeds but with words.

In the comic strip *Nancy,* the Sluggo character once said to Nancy, "That new kid in school is nothing but a big fathead!"

"You shouldn't call people names like that," Nancy replied. "I never call people names."

"Well, I just got mad when he said you were stupid-looking," Sluggo answered.

"What else did that big fathead say?" Nancy demanded.

Kindness is not softness. Kindness is not a sentimental indulgence that tolerates wrong and evil and refuses to confront a person when confrontation is required. In fact, sometimes the kindest thing you can do is confront a person about a personal fault or problem.

Suppose my doctor discovers I have a tumor. He could say to himself, "I don't want to cause this man any pain. I don't want to upset him in any way. I don't want him to leave here hurt or angry." So he brings me back into his office and says, "Everything looks great. Don't worry, be happy." That doctor is not really being kind to me; he's being unkind. To be kind, that doctor must tell me the truth and try to remove that tumor, regardless of how much it may hurt. Being kind does *not* mean being politically correct, tolerating wrongdoing, or refusing to confront a problem. Sometimes we must confront—yet in a kind way. A calm demeanor will go a lot farther than a harsh comment or an ugly tone of voice. You can make a critical point with a kind spirit, even a sense of humor.

A man was standing in line to buy an airline ticket. When he reached the counter, he said, "I would like to buy a ticket to New York City."

"No problem," said the agent. "How many pieces of luggage do you have?"

"I have three."

"Do you want to check all three to New York?"

"No, I want you to send the first suitcase to Phoenix; then send the second suitcase to Seattle, and send the third suitcase to London."

The dumbfounded clerk looked at him and said, "Sir, I'm sorry, but we can't do that."

"I don't know why not," said the man very calmly and with a smile. "That's what you did last week."

You can make your point with a butter knife just as easily as with a butcher knife.

Nice Guys Really Finish First

Aesop said, "No act of kindness, no matter how small, ever is wasted." It never pays to be unkind; it never hurts to be kind.

Remember this about kindness: It will eventually pay off for you or for someone else down the line. Kindness is never a waste of time or effort. It really is one link in an unbroken chain.

A man was driving home one evening on a small country road. Work in this small Midwestern community was almost as slow as his beat-up Pontiac, but he never quit looking for a job. Ever since his factory had closed down, he had been unemployed. And with winter coming, he had reached a point of practical desperation.

It was dark, and he almost didn't see the old lady stranded on the side of the road. But even in the dim light of day, he could see she needed help. So he pulled up in front of her Mercedes and got out. His Pontiac sputtered as he walked up to her, and he noticed that she seemed very worried. No one had stopped to help her for the last hour or so. She was wondering, *Is he going to hurt me? He doesn't look safe; he looks poor and hungry. This does not look good.* He sensed that she was frightened, standing out there alone in the cold, so he offered her some reassurance: "Ma'am, I'm just here to help you. Why don't you wait in the car where it's warm, and I'll see if I can fix your car? By the way, my name is Joe."

All she had was a flat tire, but for an old lady, that was bad enough. Joe crawled under the car, looking for a place to put the jack. He cut his hands on the hard rocks underneath the axle but was soon able to change the tire. As he was tightening up the lug nuts, she rolled down her window and began to talk to him. She told him that she was from St. Louis and was just passing through. She could not thank him enough for coming to her aid. He just smiled as he closed her trunk and started returning to his car.

"Tell me, how much do I owe you?" she asked. "I'll be glad to pay you anything you ask."

To her surprise, Joe looked back at her and said, "If you really want to pay me back, the next time you see someone who needs help, you give them the help they need, and then—just think of me." He waited until she started her car and drove off. It had been a cold and depressing day, but he felt good as he headed home in the twilight.

A few miles down the road, this same lady saw a small cafe. She went in to grab a bite to eat and take the chill off before she made the last leg of her trip home. It was a dingy-looking restaurant. One could tell business was not going well. Nevertheless, the waitress came over and brought a towel for her to wipe her wet hair. She wore a sweet smile, and even though the lady could tell the waitress was extremely tired, she was eager to please. She also noticed the waitress was nearly eight months pregnant, but neither the strain of the pregnancy nor the labor of the work changed her cheery attitude. The woman could tell her waitress was struggling just to make ends meet. She wondered how someone with so little could be so giving to a stranger. Then she thought of Joe.

After the lady finished her meal, the waitress went to get her change from a $100 bill, but the lady slipped out the door. She was gone by the time the waitress came back. The waitress wondered where the lady had gone. Then she noticed something written on a napkin, in the shape of a poem. It brought tears to her eyes. It said:

You don't owe me a thing,
I've been there too;
Someone once helped me out
The way I'm helping you.
If you really want to pay me back,
Here's what you do;
Don't let the chain of kindness
End with you.

The waitress finally made it to the end of the day. Later that night, when she got home from work and climbed into bed, she thought about the money and what the lady had written. How could the woman have known how much she and her husband needed it? With this baby coming next month, it was going to be extremely difficult, especially with her husband out of work. As she lay down in bed, she gave him a soft kiss and whispered, "Everything is going to be all right. I love you, Joe."

Take every opportunity to be kind. Ralph Waldo Emerson once said, "You cannot do a kindness too soon, for you never know how soon it will be too late."

Forget the Big Head—Have a Big Heart

The power that comes from speaking a kind word, writing a kind note, or giving a kind touch cannot be measured. It is one of the indispensable keys to being a winner and influencing anybody.

And the giver of kindness always gets more than he or she gives. The great agricultural scientist George

Washington Carver once said, "How far you go in life depends on your being tender with the young, compassionate with the aged, sympathetic with the striving, and tolerant of the weak and strong because in life you will have been all of these."

Carver's statement reminds me of former president Ronald Reagan, now suffering with the devastating illness known as Alzheimer's. Once the most powerful man in the world, he now lives in a mental prison that will ultimately take his life. Yet in his days of strength, he knew how to show kindness.

Frances Green was an eighty-three-year-old woman who lived by herself on Social Security in a rough neighborhood in Daley City, California. Though she was relatively poor, for eight years she had sent one dollar a year to the Republican National Committee.

One day she received an RNC fund-raising letter in the mail. It was beautiful, thick, and cream-colored with black and gold writing. It contained an invitation to come to the White House to meet President Reagan. What she didn't notice was the little RSVP card. Neither did she notice the suggestion that if she were going to come, she should send in a very generous donation. She thought she had been invited because they appreciated her yearly donation of a dollar.

This lady rounded up every cent that she had and took a four-day train trip to Washington, D.C. She couldn't afford a sleeper car, so she slept sitting up in the coach section. When she appeared at the appointed time at the White House gate, she presented a strange sight: a little old lady with white hair and a white-powdered face, wearing an old white suit, now yellow with age, white shoes, white stockings, and a hat older than the Great Depression. Followed by an executive with the Ford Motor Company, she walked up to the guard. As the executive watched, he sensed something amiss.

She gave her name to the guard and he looked down his list. Brusquely, he said, "Ma'am, I'm sorry, but your name isn't here and you cannot go in."

"But I was invited!" she protested. The guard wouldn't let her in, and she felt heartbroken.

The Ford executive watching all this took Frances Green aside and asked for her story. After he heard it, he said, "Stay here." He entered the White House and couldn't find anyone to help him, so he returned to her and asked, "Can you stay in Washington a day or two?"

"Well, yes," she replied, "I had planned to anyway."

"Good," he said. "Go to your hotel and meet me here at nine in the morning on Tuesday."

He was only hoping that he could do something by then. He nearly wept as he saw that heartbroken lady walking sadly away from the White House.

The man went in to Anne Higgins, a presidential aide, told her the story. Anne went to the president's secretary and told her the same story. The secretary went to President Reagan. When Reagan heard the story, he said, "When she comes next Tuesday, bring her in here."

When Tuesday arrived, it was a heavy news day, as it always is around the White House. This Ford executive knew Reagan wouldn't be able to take any time at all with Mrs. Green, but he met her at the gate, gave her a wonderful personal tour of the White House, then went by the Oval Office at the appointed time, thinking that perhaps she could get a glimpse of the president. They waited outside the Oval Office just as the National Security Council came walking out, followed by the generals of the Chief of Staff. When the executive peeked inside, Reagan gestured for him to come in. Frances Green walked in with him.

What happened next helps explain why Ronald Reagan remains one of our most beloved presidents. He knew Mrs. Green was a little old lady all by herself in the world, in many people's eyes a "nobody" with nothing to give him. He had very little to gain by seeing her. But when she walked in, he rose and called out, "Frances! Honey, forgive us, those darn computers fouled up again! If I had known you were coming, I would have come out there to get you myself."

He asked her to sit down and they talked about California, her life, and he gave her the same amount of time as if she had been the Queen of England. Though Frances Green never knew the difference, the people around Reagan knew. Big people don't have big heads, but they do have big hearts.[7]

As you travel along the road of life, you will find people weeping in the ditches of despair and the trenches of trouble, wandering the sidewalks of sorrow and suffering, walking on the detour of discouragement. As you encounter them, remember these words of Robert Prochnow:

> You may be sorry that you spoke, sorry you stayed
>   or went:
> Sorry you won or lost, sorry you thought the worst,
> Sorry so much was spent.
> But as you go through life, you'll find—
> You're never sorry you were kind.[8]

The next time you hear "Hail to the Chief," remember that regardless of who you are (or who you think you are), you can try a little kindness with everyone you meet.

PRINCIPLE FIVE

*By word or deed, take or make an opportunity
to be kind to someone today.*

How to Live the Good Life

> *There's harmony and inner peace to be found in following a moral compass that points in the same direction, regardless of fashion or trend.*
> TED KOPPEL
> ABC's *NIGHTLINE*

The French philosopher Jean Jacques Rousseau once said, "Happiness is a good bank account, a good cook, and a good digestion." Many people today would eagerly adopt Rousseau's definition of the good life.

Some say that the good life is *physical.* They believe it just doesn't get any better than a hot tub, a back rub, and a drink at the pub. Others say the good life is *material.* They think that if you've got the mansion, the Mercedes, and the money, you are living the good life.

I beg to differ. I believe the good life is *moral, ethical,* and *spiritual.* Contrary to many opinions, goodness is not feeling good, looking good, or having goods; it is *being* good and *doing* good. Goodness motivates a person to attempt to do what is best for another. It's what some might call character or integrity.

72

Goodness: The Vanishing Virtue

I have to admit a personal bias: I don't think you can talk about goodness without talking about God. If there is any meaningful standard that determines whether something is "good," that standard must be universal. Otherwise, goodness is merely a matter of opinion. A universal standard of goodness can be determined only by One who is universally good, and that One can only be God. Have you ever considered that if you take the word *God* out of the word *good*, all that's left is a big, fat zero?

The word *good* comes from an old Anglo-Saxon word with the same connotation as "God." "Good-bye" is an abbreviation of the Anglo-Saxon phrase "God be with ye." The word *good* literally means "to be like God." The word itself implies that when godliness declines, so does goodness.

On a recent trip to the nation's capital, my wife and I visited the National Archives Building to see the Declaration of Independence. We noticed that the hand-written original was extremely faded and hard to see. I remarked to my wife that I hoped as many people as possible would see it now because the ink is fading, and soon there won't be anything left to see.

Unfortunately, what is happening to this sacred and treasured document illustrates what is happening to America itself. It seems as if the principles, virtues, values, and beliefs that once seemed written on the hearts, minds, and culture of this country are fading. At this point there seems little anyone can do to stop the decay.

More than forty years ago, Robert Fitch wrote something that still remains relevant to our nation:

Ours is an age where ethics has become obsolete. It is superseded by science, deleted by philosophy, and dismissed as emotive by psychology. It drowns in compassion, evaporates into aesthetics, and retreats before relativism. The usual moral distinctions between good and bad are usually drowned in a maudlin emotion in which we feel more sympathy for the murderer than the murdered, for the adulterer than for the betrayed, and in which we have actually begun to believe that the real guilty party, the one who somehow caused it all, is the victim and not the perpetrator of the crime.[1]

Spoken more than four decades ago, these words unfortunately ring just as true today. As a baby boomer, I have witnessed how many things that once were considered either black or white have now been placed in the gray category. Goodness that used to meet a universally held standard is now a matter of personal preference. I am reminded of a poem that I read many years ago when I was in school:

When I was young and bold and strong,
Right was right, and wrong was wrong.
With plume on high and flag unfurled,
I rode away to right the world.
"Come out and fight you dogs," said I,
and wept there was but once to die.

But I am old, and good and bad
are woven in a crazy plaid.
I sit and say, "The world is so,

and he is wise who lets it go.
A battle lost, a battle won.
The difference is very small, my son."

We recently witnessed a national debate on the importance of character and goodness in the private conduct of our highest public official. One of our founding fathers, James Madison, would have felt astonishment at such a debate. The "first aim" of the Constitution, he said, was to ensure wise and virtuous rulers and to prevent what he called "their degeneracy." Consider what he avowed: "The aim of every political constitution is, or ought to be, first to obtain for rulers men who possess most wisdom to discern, and most virtue to pursue the common good of the society; and in the next place, to take the most effectual precautions for keeping them virtuous [read: good] whilst they continue to hold their public trust."[2]

The second president of the United States, John Adams, concurred. He said, "Public virtue is the only foundation of republics. There must be a positive passion for the public good, the public interest, all her power and glory established in the minds of the people, or there can be no republican government, nor any real liberty."[3]

Adams understood that public virtue depends upon private character. The lack of the latter will always lead to the demise of the former. Indeed, with a little careful thought, one can see the connection between the private character of a nation's citizens and national peace and prosperity. National prosperity largely depends upon goodness in private character.

If lying, laziness, irresponsibility, dishonesty, and corruption become commonplace, the national economy grinds down. A society that produces white-collar criminals and blue-collar predators has to pay for prison cells. A society with rampant drug abuse will have to pay for drug treatment centers. The demise of families and marriages begs for many more foster homes and lower high school graduation rates.

The less goodness there is, the more the government has to intervene—and the higher the cost of governing. Just as moral goodness leads to tremendous economic and financial benefits, the collapse of morality entails enormous financial and economic costs.[4]

The Fruit of Goodness: Doing the Right Thing

Goodness cannot exist in a vacuum, nor does it live in isolation. We measure a people's goodness by how they treat others and how they respond in situations where one action is right and the other action wrong. Good people do what is right. John Wesley, the great preacher and the founder of Methodism, said he lived by this one creed:

> Do all the good you can,
> By all the means you can,
> In all the ways you can,
> In all the places you can,
> At all the times you can,
> To all the people you can,
> As long as ever you can.[5]

What a way to live. But *why* is it always important to do that which is ethical and moral? For one thing, even though you see what you are like on the inside, the only you others see is on the outside. Proverbs 20:11 says,

"Even a child is known by his deeds, whether what he does is pure and right."

In other words, talk is cheap. No matter how much you claim to be a good person, the only public measuring stick is your actions.

You may think that by being good you're not doing a lot of good. But never underestimate the power of even one person to exert a tremendous influence by simply doing good, by simply doing the right thing at the right place and the right time.

Bob Thompson is a case in point. Taskmasters don't come much tougher than Thompson. For forty years, from April to December, he pushed his road and highway workers hard six days a week to finish the job before the first frost. Their loyalty, sweat, and hard work helped make Thompson a very rich man.

But recently Thompson returned the favor. He sold his company, Michigan's largest asphalt and paving business, and gave his 550 current and retired employees a $128 million chunk of his gains. Even workers' surviving spouses got checks. Ninety employees became instant millionaires.

Thompson started Thompson-McCully Company with $3,500 that his wife, Ellen, had earned by substitute teaching. The first five years of the business were difficult: Thompson didn't draw a salary. So why did Thompson give away so much of his fortune?

"You realize the people around you have gone through all the pain and suffering with you," he said. "I wanted to pay them back."

When the checks were handed out, Thompson stayed away. "I didn't want to be there because it gets too emotional," he admitted. But then, why did he share wealth with his workers? This was his answer: "It was the right thing to do."[6]

The Root of Goodness: Being the Right Person

Character cannot be manufactured on the outside; it emerges from what a person is on the inside. Being good is not a moonlighting occupation but a full-time job. The person of character is guided by the North Star of goodness that leads him to ask in every situation, "What is the right thing to do?"

One of my all-time heroes is the great former UCLA men's basketball coach John Wooden. He tells of center Bill Walton coming into his office at Pauley Pavilion one day with a serious question. Walton's knees had been causing him increasing pain over several months to the point that just running up and down the court hurt tremendously.

Walton walked into his mentor's office and said, "Coach, I heard that smoking marijuana will reduce the pain in my knees. Is it OK with you if I use it?"

Wooden looked up from his desk and replied, "Bill, I haven't heard that it is a pain reliever, but I have heard that it is illegal."

Classic John Wooden—right and wrong was all that mattered.[7] One of the reasons his players adore him to this day is because they saw in his heart goodness—the unquenchable desire to be the right person and to do the right thing.

One of my favorite presidents was Calvin Coolidge. When Ronald Reagan entered the White House, one of the first things he did was to put Coolidge's picture up on the wall where he could see it everyday. Calvin Coolidge probably could not be nominated, much less elected, in this telegenic age. He was a man of few words, even taciturn at times, bred of stern, puritanical New England stock. He would have shunned makeup, the one-liners, and sound bites; probably he would have been criticized for an inability to "connect" with a cutting-edge voting audience.

So why do I admire Coolidge so much? Probably because of what a reporter once said about him. In 1920, when he was mentioned for the presidential nomination, a reporter wrote this of him: "You just have confidence in Coolidge. He may not do what you want him to, he may not do what you think he ought to do, but you know *he's done his best to do right.*"[8]

What a breath of fresh air to hear a reporter say that about a politician, "You know he's done his best to do right." In my mind, that's living the good life.

Can you imagine how different our homes, businesses, schools, and government would be if we only knew we could count on others and be counted on by others to do our "best to do right." A fresh breeze of trust would blow the foul stench of cynicism to the hinterlands of our society.

Good Really Is Best

Some people think goodness is a matter of the *head.* Today every politician must give great lip service to the importance of education. They give the impression that improved education alone is the panacea for practically every problem. Yet education of the head, without an

equal emphasis on integrity of the heart, will only produce clever devils.

Robert C. Cabot of Harvard University put it well
when he wrote at the beginning of the twentieth century,
"If there is not education of men's purpose, if there is no
ethical basis at the foundation of education, then the
more we know, the smarter villains and livelier crooks we
may be. Knowledge is ethically neutral." If education
alone could solve our most perplexing problems, then
white-collar crime would cease to exist.

Others say goodness is a matter of the *hands*. They say
that goodness means treating others well. But doing good
does not make one good. Murderers on death row may be
good to their mothers, but they're not good people.

Goodness is not a matter of the head, nor a matter of
the hands; it is a matter of the *heart*. The only perfect man
who ever lived said, "A good man produces good out of
the good storeroom of his heart" (Luke 6:45). According
to Jesus Christ, goodness is not a matter of what we know
nor what we do; it is a matter of *what we are*.

Have you ever considered that a musician is judged
not by how long he plays but how well he plays? As you
think about the life ahead of you, consider that what
really matters is not how long you live but how well you
live. Sir Francis Bacon once said, "Of all virtues and dig-
nities of the mind, goodness is the greatest, being the
character of the Deity; and, without it, man is a busy, mis-
chievous, wretched thing."

My father taught me that there never is a *right* way to
do a *wrong* thing. Reuben Gonzales came to the same con-
clusion. He was in the final match of a professional rac-
quetball tournament, his first shot at a victory on the

pro circuit, and he was playing the perennial champion. In the fourth and final game, at match point, Gonzales made a super "kill" shot into the front wall to win it all. The referee called it good. One of the two linesmen affirmed that the shot was in. But Gonzales, after a moment's hesitation, turned around, shook his opponent's hand, and declared that his shot had hit the floor first. As a result, he lost the match.

He walked off the court. Everybody sat in stunned silence. Who could imagine anyone doing this in any sport? A player, with everything officially in his favor, with victory in hand, disqualified himself at match point and lost. When asked why he did it, Gonzales said, "It was the only thing I could do to maintain my integrity." Reuben Gonzales realized one of the greatest lessons we can ever learn in life—we can always win another match, but we can never regain lost integrity.[9]

Every day you will get opportunities to do a good deed, to say a good thing, to show a good heart. These days will turn into weeks, the weeks will turn into months, the months will turn into years, and the years will turn into a life. To strive for anything less than doing good and being good cheats us out of the best.

Every day you look in the mirror, consider who is looking back at you. That's the message of a powerful poem titled, "The Man in the Glass." It carries a solemn message that has stayed with me ever since I read it:

When you get what you want in your struggle for self
and the world makes you king for a day,
Just go to the mirror and look at yourself
and see what that man has to say.

For it isn't your father or mother or wife
whose judgment upon you must pass.
The fellow whose verdict counts most in your life
is the one staring back from the glass.

You may be like Jack Horner and chisel a plum
and think you're a wonderful guy.
But the man in the glass says you're only a bum
if you can't look him straight in the eye.

He's the fellow to please—never mind all the rest,
for he's with you clear to the end.
And you've passed your most dangerous, difficult
    test,
if the man in the glass is your friend.

You may fool the whole world down the pathway of
    years
and get pats on the back as you pass.
But your final reward will be heartache and tears
if you've cheated the man in the glass.

—Dale Wimbrow, 1934

When it comes to goodness, cheaters never win and
winners never cheat. Don't cheat yourself—life is too
short. Do good, be good. Be a person of character and
integrity, and you will surely live the good life.

PRINCIPLE SIX
Every day, either take the opportunity
or make the opportunity
to be the right person and do the right thing.

seven

The World's Greatest Ability

Of more than two hundred geysers in Yellowstone National Park, one stood out for many years. It was not the largest, and its waters did not reach the greatest height, but it was by far the most popular attraction. Its popularity was due to one thing alone—its *dependability*. The reason people stood in long lines under a hot sun to see it is because once every sixty-five minutes, it shot a stream of boiling water more than 170 feet into the air. One could practically set a watch by it.

One should never trouble about getting a better job, but one should do one's present job in such a manner as to qualify for a better job when it comes along.
        CALVIN
        COOLIDGE

That is why they called Old Faithful.

Many things in life could be called faithful or dependable. We depend on the sun to rise every morning and to set every night and on the tide to come in and to go out. (And we depend on the government to tax and spend, and then tax and spend some more!)

These events of nature demonstrate one of the world's greatest abilities: *dependability*. Without this ability, all other ability loses meaning. Without this ability, you will never reach your highest potential. This is the one ability that turns the ordinary into the miraculous and transforms common individuals into magnificent achievers.

A synonym for dependability is faithfulness. The wise King Solomon asked a great question in Proverbs 20:6: "Most men will proclaim each his own goodness," he said, "but who can find a faithful man?"

Employers all over the corporate world scramble to find employees who are faithful and dependable. Newlyweds expect their spouses to be faithful to their vows. Citizens want their politicians to faithfully carry out all their promises, not just "the promises they intend to keep."

Unfortunately, faithfulness appears to be another vanishing virtue in this age of quickie divorces, renegotiated contracts, and disgruntled employees.

One employee asked another, "How long have you been working for the company?"

"Ever since they threatened to fire me!" he replied.

Sadly, fear of termination motivates more employees than the joy of being faithful and dependable.

Talent on Loan from God

Are you familiar with a saying from one of the most popular radio talk show hosts in America? Rush Limbaugh begins every program by saying he has "talent on loan from God." The truth is, we *all* have talent on loan from God—or, a more familiar way of putting it, God-given talent.

All people on earth have received talents given by their

Creator—and each of these talents represents responsibilities. What is responsibility? It is our response to our God-given ability to use our abilities to the best of our ability.

Discussions of faithfulness evoke the word *duty*. Faithfulness is simply doing your duty until your duty is done. Robert E. Lee once said, "Duty is the sublimest word in our language. Do your duty in all things; you cannot do more, you should never wish to do less."

Of course, not everyone is born with equal ability. But everyone is born with an equal responsibility to use his or her abilities to the best of his or her ability. That is all any of us can do—and it is exactly what the God who gave us these abilities expects us to do.

If you are going to be faithful and dependable, you must give 100 percent of your effort 100 percent of the time in all that you do. We live in a society that merely tries to get by. If 99.9 percent does not represent your best, it is not good enough.

Insight magazine once published an article called, "Strive for Perfection . . . or Else!" According to the article, if 99.9 percent is good enough, then

- 103,260 income tax returns will be processed incorrectly this year;
- 22,000 checks will be deducted from the wrong bank accounts in the next sixty minutes;
- 1,314 phone calls will be misrouted every minute;
- twelve babies will be given to the wrong parents each day;
- 5,517,200 cases of soft drinks produced in the next twelve months will be flatter than a bad tire;
- two plane landings daily at O'Hare International Airport in Chicago will be unsafe;

- 18,322 pieces of mail will be mishandled in the next hour;
- 291 pacemaker operations will be performed incorrectly this year;
- 880,000 credit cards in circulation will turn out to have incorrect cardholder information on their magnetic strips;
- 20,000 incorrect drug prescriptions will be written in the next twelve months; and
- 107 incorrect medical procedures will be performed by the end of the day.[1]

Your best should be good enough in any situation. But nothing less than your best will ever be good enough in any situation because less than your best reflects a failure to be totally faithful and completely dependable.

Be All You Can Be

What you have, God gives you. What God gives you, you are to use. Therefore, you are accountable to use what God gives you to the best of your ability.

God has invested talents in all of us. Just as people invest in stocks and bonds, God expects a return on His investment. Do you realize that in practically every area of your life you can be faithful to use your God-given abilities for the greatest good?

We ought to be faithful, for example, in our *work*. Ecclesiastes 9:10 says, "Whatever your hand finds to do, do it with your might," which is good advice for your attitude at work. Be a faithful employee and do your best at whatever you do. Practically, that means being faithful to

- come to work on time and not leave until the workday is over;

- stay until the job is finished;
- do a job that needs to be done—even if it is not in your job description;
- give an honest day's work for an honest day's wage;
- take a lunch hour, not a three-hour paid vacation;
- report expenses accurately and truthfully; and
- uphold the team and the company's reputation.

This kind of faithfulness might revolutionize a lot of companies and corporations.

We also ought to be faithful with our *wealth*. We live in the most prosperous nation in the world. Even the less financially privileged in this country are rich compared to the average person in many other countries. As you think about the money you make and the possessions you have, consider the following:

- Do you spend money exclusively on yourself, or do you invest some of it in the lives of others?
- If all the charities in America and the world were supported by your charitable giving, how many charities would be left?
- Do you see all of your money as a blessing for you to enjoy alone, or do you see a part of your money as a blessing to share with others?

Do you apply the same standards of faithfulness and dependability to your work life, spiritual life, financial life, and family life that you apply to other areas of your life? For example:

- If your car starts once every three times, would you call it reliable?
- If your newspaper is not delivered every Monday and Thursday, would you consider the delivery service trustworthy?

- If you skip work once or twice a month under false pretenses, would you say you are a loyal employee?
- If your refrigerator stops working for a day every now and then, do you say, "Oh well, it works most of the time"?
- If your water heater provides an icy cold shower every once in awhile, would you be satisfied with its dependability?
- If you miss a couple of loan payments every year, does the bank say, "Well, ten out of twelve isn't bad"?

We ought to be faithful to our word. I was reared the old-fashioned way, and I thank God for my dad, who is now in heaven, for the upbringing he gave me. One of the things Dad taught me was that I was no better than my word. I still believe that the weakest handshake should be better than the strongest ink on any contract. Have you ever considered that your word is the only thing not worth giving unless you keep it?

You are not accountable for being *the* best, but you are accountable for being *your* best.

If you can't be a highway, then just be a trail;
If you can't be the sun, be a star;
It isn't by size that you win or you fail—
Be the best of whatever you are.

—Douglas Malloch

Dependability Even in the Little Things Is a Big Thing

How can you develop the virtues of faithfulness and dependability in your life? Begin with the little things.

Dependability begins, grows, and matures by being faithful to the little things.

Too many people today think they are too big for the small things; they would rather get on with what they believe are the bigger things in life. Longfellow once said, "Most people would succeed in small things if they were not troubled with great ambition."

A man was talking to a strapping giant of a fellow. "If I were as big, tall, and strong as you," he said, "I would go out in the woods, find the biggest bear I could find, and wrestle him right down to the ground."

The big man just looked at him and said, "There are plenty of little bears in the woods."

I have heard people say, "If I had a million dollars, there are so many things I would do for other people and for God." That simply isn't so. The truth is, we would do the same thing with a million dollars that we would do with a hundred dollars.

Faithfulness can turn even a menial job into a vitally important task. Just recently I came across a great illustration of this principle. The following is a simple definition of dependability and faithfulness. If you can't guess what it is, see the answer at the end of the chapter.

I represent my country.
I'm always ready for service.
I go wherever I'm sent.
I do what I'm asked to do.
I stick to my task until it's done.
I don't strike back when I'm struck.
I don't give up when I'm licked.
I keep up-to-date.

I find no job too small.
I work well on a team for big jobs.
I'm crowned with a mark of service.

If you haven't figured out what it is, go ahead and sneak a peek at the end of the chapter.

Moments to Millennia

We have recently entered a new millennium. But have you ever pondered what a millennium is? A millennium is made up of centuries; centuries are made up of decades; decades are made up of years; years are made up of months; months are made up of weeks; weeks are made up of days; days are made up of hours; hours are made up of minutes; minutes are made up of seconds or moments. Think about it—it's the little things (moments) that make up the big things (millennia).

For example, the other day I asked my beautiful wife if she married me for my looks.

"No, I didn't marry you for your looks," she replied. "I married you for your brains—it's the little things that count." (Just kidding—my darling wife never puts me down like that. Besides, I showed how big my brains are by marrying her!)

I'm a big sports fan, and one of my favorite sports is baseball. Every baseball fan likes a "clutch hitter," the player who wins the game with a crucial hit in the last few innings. We tend to admire certain ballplayers who seem to regularly pull the game out of the fire. But amazingly, statistics reveal such players exist only in our minds.

Studies done by pioneer baseball analyst Bill James and researchers for Stats Incorporated have determined that the phenomenon of clutch hitters is simply a myth. Allen Barra and Allen Schwarz, sportswriters for the *Wall Street Journal,* have noted that "what a hitter does in most clutch situations is pretty much what he does all the rest of the time." The statistics even reveal the top hitters in baseball actually average a thirteen-point *drop* in their batting average when the game is close in the late innings.

What occurs on the baseball diamond is no different from what happens in every aspect of life. When things get tough, the person who comes through is generally the same person who *consistently* comes through when things aren't so tough. In other words, when the game is on the line, it's the dependable person you want up to bat.[2]

Faithfulness Is Job One

Aaron Feuerstein owns a company called Malden Mills. On December 31, 1995, he was celebrating his seventieth birthday when he got an urgent call to rush to his company. When he arrived, he saw that his factory had caught fire and burned to the ground.

This was no ordinary company. It was a 130-year-old textile company in Lawrence, Massachusetts, founded by Feuerstein's grandfather. The fire had reduced three of its factories, covering an area about the size of a track field, to nothing but charred metal and brick.

Where ninety-nine out of one hundred people would have fallen into total despair, Feuerstein held on to a remote possibility. He noticed the flames had not reached the building that housed the key production unit. As he watched firefighters try to put out the blaze, he turned to his director of engineering and said, "If they can save that building, the mill can stay in business."

The executive replied, "You're just dreaming, Aaron."

This factory employed thirty-four hundred workers and was the main employer for two neighboring towns. All the workers believed it was the end of their jobs. All Feuerstein had to do was take the $300 million in insurance money and call it quits, and he would be set for life.

But an amazing thing happened.

While the smoke still rose from the charred remains of the fire, Feuerstein called his workers together at a school gymnasium. They were about to discover what kind of a man they worked for. He announced that he was not going to abandon them—that he was going to rebuild the factory. More than that, he was going to keep all thirty-four hundred of them on the payroll for one month . . . and give each of them a $275 Christmas bonus.

As it happened, all Malden Mill employees received full pay and benefits for *three* months after the fire. All Feuerstein asked in return was their best efforts to rebuild the business.

Just three months later, two of Malden Mill's three divisions were running again at near full capacity. Eighty percent of the firm's employees were back at work. Even though it cost him $1.5 million a week to pay the salaries, and the hospitalization insurance of his employees, the owner kept his word. In fact, Feuerstein estimates that it cost $10 million to pay his workers who lost their jobs from the fire for ninety days, plus full health-care benefits for 180 days.

Did the investment pay off? The quality and efficiency of production surpassed its prefire standards. In just one of the rebuilt plants alone, the production of fabric doubled its previous output. Before the fire, 6 to 7 percent of the manufactured products failed to meet quality requirements; after the fire, that number dropped to 2 percent. When the employees were asked to name the key to the turnaround, they all agreed: "It was the faithfulness and loyalty of Aaron Feuerstein."[3]

Always Faithful

More than two hundred years ago when the United States Marine Corp first formed, officials gave much time to considering an appropriate motto. They finally chose the Latin phrase *Semper Fidelis,* a phrase today engraved on the mind of every United States marine. What does it mean? *Always faithful.*

Those are two very important words, but the more important of the two is the first. Why? Because it explains how a marine is to be faithful. A marine is not to be faithful only when it is convenient, when he feels like it, or when it will make him happy. *Semper Fidelis* means *always* faithful—regardless of the cost. That's why the world's greatest ability is indeed dependability.

(The answer to the puzzle asked earlier: I am a postage stamp.)

PRINCIPLE SEVEN
*Take every opportunity today
to be faithful and dependable,
to do your best and be your best.*

The Lower You Get, the Higher You Go

> *Talent is God-given, be humble; Fame is man-given, be thankful; Conceit is self-given, be careful.*
> JOHN WOODEN

A fifth-grader came home from school, bubbling with excitement after being voted "Prettiest Girl in the Class." She was even more excited when she came home the next day after the class voted her the "Most Popular Person in the Class."

Several days later she won a third contest, but she said nothing about it. Her mother noted her silence and asked, "What were you voted this time?"

"Most Stuck-Up," she said in barely a whisper.

At times we all get too stuck on ourselves. It is difficult to keep the hot air of selfishness and pride from over-inflating our sense of importance. At the least insult or slightest remark, we're ready to sue for millions, spout and fume, and gripe and complain as though our children had just been drawn and quartered.

A New National Motto

We've all heard what I believe has become the new national motto. It used to be "In God We Trust"; today it is "I Want My Rights."

These days you can't turn right without running into someone's rights. Rights are demanded for children, the elderly, the disabled, workers under twenty-five, workers over forty, alcoholics, the addicted, the homeless, spotted owls, snail darters—in essence, for everybody except the unborn.

Rights are considered as American as apple pie. Indeed, this is a country known for citizens' rights. The best-known part of our Constitution is the Bill of Rights. Rights provide the bedrock of our society, and we should give our lives to defend them. They spell freedom. It is because of our rights that we are not run by an autocratic government. But as Philip K. Howard says in his great book *The Death of Common Sense:*

> Rights have taken on a new role in America. Whenever there is a perceived injustice, new rights are created to help the victims. These rights are different: while the rights-bearers may see them as "protection," they don't protect so much as provide.
>
> These rights are intended as a new, and often invisible, form of subsidy. They are provided at everyone else's expense, but the amount of the check is left blank. . . . Rights, however, leave no room for balance, or for looking at it from everybody's point of view as well. Rights, as the legal

philosopher Ronald Dworkin has noted, are a trump card. Rights give open-ended power to one group and it comes out of everybody else's hide.[1]

So what has the rights movement fostered? A spirit of anything except gentleness, humility, or courtesy.

Instead, people are encouraged to "look out for number one" and to get what they want through intimidation. But winners don't have to intimidate. In fact, intimidation is for losers.

A Kinder, Gentler You

One of the keys in getting along with others is *first getting along with yourself.* You cannot see others properly until you see *yourself* properly. When George H. W. Bush was inaugurated as president of the United States, he said he wanted America to become a "kinder, gentler nation."

Someone has well said, "Nothing is so strong as gentleness; nothing so gentle as real strength." Just as you catch more flies with honey than with vinegar, so people respond far more readily to gentleness than to intimidation.

Coach John Wooden tells the following story that illustrates a great truth:

> My dad, Joshua Wooden, was a strong man in one sense but a gentle man. While he could lift heavy things men half his age couldn't lift, he would also read poetry to us each night after a day working in the fields raising corn, hay, wheat, tomatoes, and watermelons.

We had a team of mules named Jack and Kate on our farm. Kate would often get stubborn and lie down on me when I was plowing. I couldn't get her up no matter how roughly I treated her. Dad would see my predicament and walk across the field until he got close enough to say, "Kate." Then she would get up and start working again. He never touched her in anger.

It took me a long time to understand that even a stubborn mule responds to gentleness.[2]

What is true of a mule is true of people. This is exactly what Jesus Christ meant when He said in the Sermon on the Mount, "Blessed are the meek, for they shall inherit the earth" (Matt. 5:5 NKJV). The word *meek* refers to a kind, gentle spirit. (Incidentally, it's too bad that the meek have not already inherited the earth because the unmeek are making a real mess of it.)

Of course, when I speak of gentleness and meekness and humility, I do not mean *weakness.* Meekness is not weakness, and gentleness is not wimpishness. The words *meekness* or *gentleness* should not conjure up the image of a short, skinny nerd with thick glasses who sings soprano in the church choir. Meekness means *power under control.* An unbroken horse is useless; an overdose of medicine kills rather than cures; wind out of control destroys everything in its path.

A Lesson from Gentle Ben

Think of meekness as *the security to practice humility.* When Benjamin Franklin was twenty-two years old, he was living in Philadelphia after escaping an oppressive apprenticeship. He was, as they say, trying to find himself. One question burned in his heart: "What are the greatest priorities of my life?"

In answer Franklin developed twelve "virtues"— the values that would govern his life. They were temperance, silence, order, resolution, frugality, industry, sincerity, justice, moderation, cleanliness, tranquility, and chastity.

Franklin took these twelve virtues to a Quaker friend and asked his opinion. The friend looked at them and said, "Benjamin, you have forgotten the most important one."

Franklin was aghast. "Which one?" he asked.

The old Quaker replied, *"Humility."*

Franklin immediately added this thirteenth virtue and then organized his life into thirteen weekly cycles, determining that for one week out of thirteen he would try to focus on one of those virtues.

When he reached seventy-eight years of age, he began looking back on his life and considering the qualities he had built his life around. Though he felt pretty good about having achieved most of them, concerning humility he said, "I cannot boast of much success in acquiring the *reality* of this virtue; but I had a good deal with regard to the *appearance* of it."[3]

I can understand why Franklin felt this way. Humility is one of the greatest virtues and character traits known to man—and one of the most elusive. Think about it: We're supposed to show it but *not know it.* In fact, if we *try* to be humble, we have fooled ourselves into thinking we have something to be humble about.

I think of the young, gifted minister who was indeed a good preacher. As his congregation began to grow, so did his head. After he had delivered his latest masterpiece, a church member shook his hand and said, "You are, without a doubt, one of the greatest preachers of our generation." It was all the minister could do to squeeze his head into the car as he slid behind the steering wheel. As he and his wife drove back home, he relayed what the church member had said to him. She did not respond.

After futilely fishing for affirmation, he finally looked over at his wife and said, "I wonder just how many 'great preachers' there are in this generation?"

Without a smile, his wife replied, "One fewer than you think, my dear."

Humility is indispensable in developing a gentle, gracious spirit. It is only when we deflate our self-importance and inflate the importance of others that we will treat others the way they deserve to be treated.

The Most Important Musical Instrument

Someone once asked Leonard Bernstein, the late New York Symphony conductor, what the most difficult position in the orchestra was. Without hesitation, the great maestro replied, "Second fiddle." Everyone wants to sit in the first chair, not the second.

This is true not only in orchestra but in any relationship. For twenty-five years I have been married to the most beautiful, wonderful woman I have ever known. We have had our ups and downs, our peaks and valleys, good times and not so good. But I have learned (and am still learning) that when I play "second fiddle," she winds up putting me in the first chair.

Sometimes, however, I make the mistake of the husband who, in the middle of a sharp argument with his wife, finally said in disgust, "OK, I'll meet you halfway. I will admit I'm right if you'll admit you're wrong." Trust me, such a response will only get you halfway out the door.

Whether it is your spouse, your secretary, or your next-door neighbor, everyone hungers for and responds to those who offer courtesy and gentleness in a spirit of humility.

When Ronald Reagan was governor of California, he gathered up his belongings and left the office early one day. Michael Deaver, one of his assistants, asked him why he was leaving so soon.

"I've just got a few errands to run," he replied.

Deaver said this would happen occasionally, and it would always make him curious. On this day he pulled Reagan's driver, Dale, aside and told him he wanted a report the next day on exactly what Reagan had done.

After Reagan left, Deaver looked through the "to read" file that sat on his desktop. On top of the pile was a wrinkled letter from a man stationed in Vietnam. The soldier had written a letter to Governor Reagan, telling him about life in Southeast Asia and how much he missed his wife. He felt miserable and just wanted to tell his wife how much he loved her and how he wanted to be with her. That day was their wedding anniversary and they would be separated. Although the man reported that he had already sent a card, he asked the governor if he could put in a phone call to make sure his wife was OK. He wanted the governor to pass on his love, just in case she didn't receive his card.

The next day, Dale told Deaver that Reagan had done more than what the soldier had requested. The governor picked up a dozen red roses and personally delivered them to the soldier's wife. Dale reported that Reagan approached the woman in an extremely humble way, offering the flowers on behalf of a loving husband stationed in a jungle hell thousands of miles away on the other side of the world. Then he spent more than an hour with the woman, drinking coffee and talking about her family.[4] Maybe that was one of the secrets to the enduring popularity of Ronald Reagan.

Gentle on My Mind

Do you know how two goats respond when they meet each other in a narrow path above a stream of water? They cannot turn back and they cannot pass each other for they lack even an inch of spare room. Instinctively they know if they butt each other, both will fall into the water and drown. So what do those goats do?

Nature has taught one goat to lie down so that the other can pass over its body; as a result, each goat arrives at its destination safe and sound.

Zig Ziglar is fond of saying, "You can have everything you want in life if you will just help enough other people to get what they want." My version of his proverb: "Treat others with the respect that they deserve, and they will in turn elevate you higher than you could ever go on your own."

The Hole in the Water

Whenever you feel an inflated sense of your own importance, you might want to remember the following poetic truth. It applies no matter how far up the ladder you have climbed.

Sometimes when you're feeling important,
Sometimes when your ego's in bloom,
Sometimes when you take it for granted that
You're the best-qualified in the room,

Sometimes when you feel that your going
Would leave an unfillable hole,
Just follow this simple instruction
And see how it humbles your soul.

Take a bucket and fill it with water,
Put your hand in it, up to the wrist,
Then pull it out, and the hole that's remaining
Is a measure of how you'll be missed.

You may splash all you please when you enter,
You can stir up the water galore,
But stop and you'll find in a minute
That it looks quite the same as before.

The moral on this quaint example
Is do the best that you can,
Be proud of yourself but remember,
There is no indispensable man.

—Ogden Nash

Principle Eight
Always make people you deal with feel as if they are more important than you—and treat them accordingly.

Never Let Them See You Sweat

A flight instructor was sitting next to his student in their single-engine plane. "Well," he said, "I think it's time to take her in for a landing. Are you ready to go down?"

"No problem," said the student. "Let's do it."

> *He that would govern others, first must govern himself.*
> PHILIP MASSINGER

As they approached the runway, the instructor looked at his student and noticed his absolute calm. Normally, students coming in for their first landing were nervous, wide-eyed, and sweaty. But this young man looked as cool as the underside of a pillow. The instructor thought, *I cannot believe how calm this young man is. He will make a great pilot.*

Suddenly the plane hit the runway with a thud, bounced fifty feet into the air, hit and bounced again, ran off the runway, and landed upside down in a cornfield. The instructor, upside down and still strapped in his seat, exclaimed, "Son, that was the worst first landing any student of mine has ever made."

"Me?" asked the student. "I thought *you* were landing the plane."

That young pilot may not have been in control of the plane, but he was in control of himself. The extraordinary trait of self-control allows you to stay in control when everything else is not.

When the Control Button Is Off

Today's tree of culture is mostly barren of the fruit of self-control. We live in a society increasingly out of control.

Our society is *financially* out of control. Americans are the most indebted people on earth, with household debt averaging $71,500—*twice* that of Great Britain and *eighty-nine* times that of Switzerland.[1] Our nation's credit card debt alone dwarfs the gross national product of many small countries.

Many Americans are like professional golfer Doug Sanders, who once said, "I'm working as hard as I can to get my life and my cash to run out at the same time. If I can die right after lunch on Tuesday, everything will be fine."

Our society is also *physically* out of control. Did you know that every day in America, we eat

- seventy-five acres of pizza
- 53 million hot dogs
- 167 million eggs
- 3 million gallons of ice cream
- three thousand tons of candy

In addition we spend

- $2,021,918 on exercise equipment
- $3,561,644 on tortilla chips
- $10,410,959 on potato chips

Every day, Americans drink 524 million servings of Coca-Cola and eat 2,739,726 Dunkin Donuts. Still, 101,280,321 adults are on diets.[2]

California pathologist Thomas J. Bassier has noticed that in the autopsies he has performed, two out of every three deaths are premature, related to what he calls "loafer's heart," "smoker's lung," and "drinker's liver."[3]

Recent studies from the Centers for Disease Control in Atlanta say that nearly 60 percent of adults do not exercise regularly.[4] The word *exercise,* like the word *discipline,* really irritates some people. One man said, "Whenever I think about exercising, I just sit down and rest until the feeling goes away." And that is precisely why many people die sooner rather than later.

Our society is *emotionally* out of control. Our highways have become battlegrounds and our schoolyards shooting fields. Road rage is now *the* rage on the highway. Airline rage, grocery store rage, and youth sport rage are being reported by the media with unprecedented frequency. If we blow our horns at a stranger, he may use us for target practice. And children are now shooting children, as well as teachers, for almost no reason at all.

James Garbarino, human development professor at Cornell University, reports a major social shift: "There is a general breakdown of social conventions, of manners, of social controls. This gives a validation, a permission, to be aggressive. Kids used to be guided by a social convention that said, 'Keep the lid on.' Today they are guided more in the direction of taking it off."[5]

Garbarino also observes an increasing "culture of vulgarity." Obscenities are now common on cable TV, while violence is promoted in much of today's music.

Psychologist Frank Farley of Temple University is concerned about "a loosening of inhibitions promoted on TV talk shows such as Jerry Springer's [in which] it is OK to say whatever is on your mind."[6]

It naturally follows from all this to expect a society that is *morally* out of control. In a September 20, 1998, ABC's news magazine show *20/20* reporter John Stossel interviewed Dr. Roy Baumeister of Case Western University. Baumeister said, "If you look at the social and personal problems facing people in the United States—we're talking drug and alcohol abuse, teen pregnancy, unsafe sex, school failure, shopping problems, gambling—over and over, the majority of them have self-control failure as central to them. Studies show that self-control does predict success in life over a very long time."

Without question, we are reaping the bitter fruit of the "let it all hang out" mentality of the sixties and seventies, in which self-control became the *persona non grata* of an entire generation. The effects are felt not only here but abroad. Alan Widdecomb, Shadow Home Secretary in the British House of Commons, admits, "Let's face it, we are not a happier society as a result of the liberalisation of the seventies. We have record rates of suicides, record rates of teenage pregnancy, record rates of youth crime, record rates of underage sex. We should invite people to recognize that the Great Experiment has failed. *You cannot have happiness without restraint.*"[7]

Our culture reminds me of a man who bumped into an acquaintance in a bar and remarked, "I thought you'd given up drinking. What's the matter—no self-control?"

"Sure, I've got plenty of self-control," he replied. "I'm just too strong to use it."

Whether it's playing a musical instrument, mastering a computer program, or learning a foreign language, any worthwhile endeavor demands self-control. Perhaps that is why Aristotle called self-control "the hardest victory." He also said, "I count him braver who overcomes his desires than him who conquers his enemies." Self-control is the difference between victory and defeat in the game of life. Those who control self, win; those who don't, lose.

You Are Just Too Much

Though it is true that you will never be free *of* self, you must be free *from* self if you are going to be a winner and influence others in a positive way. Either you control self or self will control you.

We live in a society saturated with self. Listen to a few book titles from both religious and secular bookstores that are selling like hotcakes: *Love Yourself; The Art of Learning to Love Yourself; Loving Yourselves; Celebrate Yourself; You're Something Special; Self-Esteem: You're Better Than You Think; Talking to Yourself: Learning the Language of Self-Affirmation;* and finally, *Self-Esteem: The New Reformation.*

Psychiatrists and psychoanalysts have in recent years promoted a movement known as "Selfism," which elevates self to the level of god and seeks to avoid anything that would lower someone's self-esteem. Over the last couple of decades, the lexicon of "self" words has been purged of all terms that "selfists" regard as negative. They urge the eradication of words such as self-criticism, self-denial, self-discipline, self-control, self-mastery, self-effacement, self-reproach, or self-sacrifice. They encourage the use of words such as self-confidence, self-contentment, self-expression, self-assertion, self-indulgence, self-realization, self-approval, self-actualization, and even self-worship.

Selfism has one commandment: "I am the lord *my* god; I shall not have strange gods before me."[8]

We see this self-emphasis even in our daily speech. If you are like most Americans, you know ten thousand to twenty thousand words (out of a possible six hundred thousand English words), but you use only five thousand to ten thousand words in everyday conversation.

Twenty-five percent of average American speech is made up of ten basic words. A mere fifty words make up 60 percent of our speaking vocabulary. The most common words are *you, the,* and *a;* but the most common word is *I.* As Pogo said, "We have met the enemy, and the enemy is us."

I'm not denigrating the need for a healthy self-image. Indeed, that quality is indispensable to the virtue of self-control, for only those who see themselves as they should will be motivated to control themselves as they ought. Yet an unhealthy preoccupation with one's self can turn into a selfish desire to gratify the ego at all times and all costs. And *that* can be the death knell of meaningful relationships and effective leadership.

It's Cool to Be Cool

Are you ready for another story from coach John Wooden? If anyone in all of sports ever set a multiplicity of records that may never be broken, it was John Wooden. From 1948 to 1975, he had a win-loss record of 885-203—a phenomenal career winning percentage of .813. He directed an eighty-eight-game winning streak and won ten national championships in twelve years.

Wooden obviously knew what it was to be in high-pressure situations, but he was the antithesis of many of today's profanity-spouting, chair-throwing, red-faced, tie-loosening, fast-pacing, ear-rattling coaches on the sidelines.

He seldom left his seat on the bench, never uttered a profanity (he did utter a "goodness gracious alive" occasionally), never screamed or went on a tirade. Usually he just sat calmly on the bench with his program rolled up in his hand, occasionally giving instructions in a cool, collected manner. Listen to his reasoning: "I tried to teach players that if they lose their temper or get out of control, they will get beat." He added, "Modeling was better than words. I liked the rule that we used to have that a coach couldn't leave the bench. I'm sorry they did away with that."[9]

Wooden gained fame for something else—his formula for success in life, known as the "pyramid of success." He coined his own definition of success: "Peace of mind which is a direct result of self-satisfaction in knowing you made the effort to do the best of which you are capable." (At the risk of presumption, I would offer my version, which ends with "the effort to *be* the best of which you are capable"—I don't think Coach Wooden would disagree.) To visually show how this success is achieved, Wooden spent fourteen years developing the "pyramid."

One of Wooden's building blocks in his pyramid was self-control, which the coach valued to "practice self-discipline and keep emotions under control [since] good judgment and common sense are essential." People who exhibit this common thread of self-control are successful in life.

This fact has been clinically proven. In the 1960s researchers at Stanford University ran the "candy test." They put a large group of four-year-olds in a room and had a teacher tell them, "I am leaving for ten minutes to run an errand. Here are two pieces of candy you may have while I am gone, but if you wait until I return, you can have ten pieces of candy." They wanted to know who had the self-control to resist temptation and hold out for the full reward.

After a dozen years, they restudied the same children. They found that those who grabbed the two pieces of candy tended to be more troubled as adolescents and scored an average of 210 points less on SAT tests than the others. The boys who exhibited self-control had fewer run-ins with the law, and their counterparts among the girls were less likely to get pregnant out of wedlock.[10]

Self-control is a key factor in whether we will be successful. We can't control everything in life, but if there is one thing we can and must control, it is the self. Dr. Baumeister, the expert interviewed on *20/20,* added, "If we're concerned about raising children to be successful and healthy and happy, forget about self-esteem. *Concentrate on self-control.*"

You Are Either in Control or Out of Control

In countless areas, self-control is vital to being a winner and influencing anybody. Here's why.

First, winners control their *time.* Without question, the last year has been the most stressful, pressure-packed of my life. In the last twelve months, I have served as president of the Southern Baptist Convention, built a new home while selling and moving from an old one, traveled to South and Central America and Africa, spoken all over the country, and written this book.

That doesn't take into account golf lessons, serving on the boards of a nationwide TV ministry and a major university, pastoring a great church, preparing weekly sermons, and reading several periodicals and books weekly. That leaves out my most important roles: being the husband of the greatest wife and the father of the greatest sons in the world.

I have been forced to control my time . . . or die. I cannot tell you the number of times people have said to me, "I am sorry to bother you; I know your time is so valuable." Listen, everybody's time is valuable. No one has any more or less time than you have. The discipline and stewardship of our time is important because our management of time is the management of self.

Believe it or not, time management is not complicated. For years I have made out a list of things I needed to get done, prioritized them in order of importance, and as much as possible, worked my plan, taking one task at a time. Regardless of how you do it, as Nike says, "Just do it!"

Peter Drucker is one of the most respected mentors of winners and influencers in America. He has said many great things but none more profound than this: "Nothing else perhaps distinguishes effective executives as much as their tender, loving care of time. . . . Unless he manages himself effectively, no amount of ability, skill, experience, or knowledge will make an executive effective."[11]

My good buddy Zig Ziglar says, "If you will do what you ought to do when you ought to do it, the day will come when you can do what you want to do when you want to do it." Self-control is just that—postponing the impulsive pleasure for the important task. Consider the following little couplet:

> If you would live your life with ease:
> do what you ought, not what you please.

Winners also control their *tongues*. Nothing can betray you so quickly as a slip of the tongue. James 3:6 says, "The tongue is a fire." What awesome power this little member of our body has.

More than a thousand firefighters battled a wildfire for two weeks in the Black Hills of North Dakota. The fire started on August 24, 2000, and was not contained until September 8. In those few days, more than eighty thousand acres of prime timberland burned up.

The cause? Apparently a forty-six-year-old woman stopped on a deserted road that fateful August day, lit a cigarette, and tossed the still-burning match on the ground. Rather than put out the fire, she decided to leave the area. She faces up to five years in prison and $250,000 in fines—but the damage has been done.[12]

In the same way, a rumor, half-truth, sarcastic remark, or angry rejoinder can turn into a lit match capable of burning down acres of office morale, marital harmony, and family unity. Dewey Knight, former assistant county manager of Dade County, Florida, once said, "My best advice came from a friend immediately after I was named to a top county job: 'Son, in this job you will have millions of opportunities to keep your mouth shut. Take advantage of all of them.'" Great advice when you remember you never have to apologize for something you don't say.

Finally, winners control their *tempers.* Red hair, Italian ancestors, or even the stupidity of others is no excuse for a short fuse or explosive temper. Do you realize that no one can make you *lose* your temper? Others can only prompt you to *find* it (and make you wish later that you hadn't). Someone has well said that your temper is so valuable that you should keep it, not lose it.

It was a hot, humid day in Kansas City. The eight-hour shift seemed especially long for the veteran bus driver. Suddenly a young female passenger, apparently upset about something, let loose with a string of profane words. The bus driver, looking in his overhead mirror, could sense everyone around her felt embarrassed by the obscenities.

A few blocks later, still mumbling, the angry passenger began to disembark. As she stepped down, the bus driver calmly said, "Madam, I believe you're leaving something behind."

"Oh?" she snapped. "And what is that?"

"A very bad impression," the bus driver responded.

The King in You

Someone has said, "Winners are those who can stay cool in a hot place, sweet in a sour place, and little in a big place." That is the force and power of self-control.

Frederick the Great of Prussia was walking on the outskirts of Berlin when he encountered a very old man moving in the opposite direction.

"Old man," Frederick said, "who are you?"

"Why, I am a king," the old man replied.

Frederick laughed. "A king!" he said. "Over what kingdom do you reign?"

"Over myself," the old man proudly replied.

Ronald Reagan once rightly said, "If no one among us is capable of governing himself, then who among us has the capacity to govern someone else?"

The British poet Rudyard Kipling captured the essence of self-control in one of the greatest poems ever written, "If."

> If you can keep your head when all about you
> Are losing theirs and blaming it on you;
> If you can trust yourself when all men doubt you,
> But can make allowance for their doubting too;
> If you can wait and not be tired by waiting,
> Or, being lied about, don't deal in lies,
> Or, being hated, don't give way to hating,
> And yet don't look too good, nor talk too wise;
>
> If you can dream—and not make dreams your master;
> If you can think—and not make thoughts your aim;
> If you can meet with triumph and disaster
> And treat those two imposters just the same;
> If you can bear to hear the truth you've spoken,
> Twisted by knaves to make a trap for fools,
> Or watch the things you gave your life to broken,
> And stoop and build 'em up with worn-out tools;
>
> If you can make one heap of all your winnings
> And risk it on one turn of pitch-and-toss,
> And lose, and start again at your beginnings
> And never breathe a word about your loss;
> If you can force your heart and nerve and sinew
> To serve your turn long after they are gone,

And so hold on when there is nothing in you
Except the Will which says to them: "Hold on";

If you can talk with crowds and keep your virtue,
Or walk with kings—nor lose the common touch;
If neither foes nor loving friends can hurt you;
If all men count with you, but none too much;
If you can fill the unforgiving minute
With sixty seconds' worth of distance run—
Yours is the Earth and everything that's in it,
And—which is more—you'll be a Man, my son![13]

Winners respond in all situations according to principle and sound judgment, rather than according to impulse, selfish desire, or social custom. As a winner, make a commitment to self-control today.

PRINCIPLE NINE

Respond according to principle and what is right.
Don't react to the actions of others.

The Right Connection

> *What lies behind us and what lies before us are tiny matters compared to what lies within us.*
> RALPH WALDO EMERSON

Larry Walters drove a truck for a living, but all his life he had dreamed of flying. After graduating from high school, he joined the air force, hoping to become a pilot, but his poor eyesight disqualified him. When he finally left the military, he had to content himself with watching others fly fighter jets over his backyard. Day after day he sat in his lawn chair, dreaming about the magic of flying.

Then one day Walters got an idea. He visited the local Army-Navy Surplus store and bought a tank of helium and forty-five weather balloons—heavy-duty spheres that measured more than four feet across when fully inflated.

Back in his yard, Walters attached the balloons to his aluminum lawn chair with straps. He anchored the chair to the bumper of his Jeep and inflated the balloons with helium. Then he packed some sandwiches and drinks and

116

loaded a BB gun, figuring he could pop a few of the balloons when it was time to return to earth.

When all seemed ready, Walters sat down in his chair and cut the anchoring cord. He thought he would rise lazily for a couple hundred feet, spend a few minutes looking around the neighborhood, then drift gently back down to earth.

Things didn't quite work out that way.

When Walters cut the cord, he didn't lazily float up; he shot up as if he had been fired out of a cannon. And he didn't rise only a couple hundred feet; he climbed to eleven thousand feet. At that height he couldn't risk deflating any of the balloons because he might unbalance the load and *really* do some flying. So he sailed among the clouds for fourteen hours at eleven thousand feet in a lawn chair. He had no clue how to get down.

Eventually, Larry drifted into the approach corridor for the Los Angeles International Airport. A Pan Am pilot radioed the air traffic control tower and said, "You won't believe this, but I've just passed a guy in a lawn chair at eleven thousand feet with a BB gun in his lap."

The Los Angeles International Airport sits right on the ocean. At nightfall the winds along the coast begin to change. Those winds began to carry Larry out to sea. At that point, the navy dispatched a helicopter to rescue him, but the rescue team had a hard time reaching him because the draft from the rotor kept pushing his balloons farther out to sea. Eventually, pilots were able to hover over him, drop a rescue line, and haul him to safety.

Police arrested Walters as soon as he hit the ground. While officers led him away in handcuffs, a television reporter called out, "Mr. Walters, why did you do it?"

Walters stopped, eyed the man, and said, "A man just can't sit around."[1]

Even though there are better ways to make the point, Mr. Walters had it right: There is far more to life than just sitting around, doing nothing. You have the God-given potential to be all that you can be.

John Maxwell, recognized as one of the foremost experts on leadership today, has defined leadership as "influence." If you will put into practice the principles found in this book, you will certainly have influence—but more than just influence, the positive influence of a winner.

Help Is on the Way

How can anyone display all of these qualities consistently? Humanly speaking, you can't. That's the bad news. The good news is, it is not only a possibility but distinct reality—*if you have the right connection.*

A five-year-old boy fell out of bed, waking the entire household with his cry. After his mother had safely tucked him back under the covers, she asked, "Why did you fall out of bed?"

Between tears and sobs, he said, "Well, I guess I went to sleep too close to where I got in."

Too many people do just that in life—sleepwalk too close to where they began. So they fall far short of what God created them to become.

The vast majority of people never learn the secret of how to become a winner who can influence anybody. I didn't randomly pick out the nine qualities we've discussed. These virtues are *fruit*—the fruit of the Holy Spirit. The Bible says that "the fruit of the Spirit is love, joy, peace, long-suffering, kindness, goodness, faithful-ness, gentleness, [and] self-control" (Gal. 5:22–23 NKJV).

These virtues are not naturally manufactured—they are *supernaturally produced.* Those who have God's Holy Spirit living in them have the supernatural ability to be winners who can influence anybody. All it takes is the *right connection.*

The Fruit Comes from the Root

Jesus revealed the secret connection in a talk He once gave to His disciples. "I am the true vine, and My Father is the vinedresser . . . I am the vine, you are the branches. He who abides in Me, and I in him, bears much fruit; for without me you can do nothing" (John 15:1, 5 NKJV). Keep in mind that, horticulturally speaking, the *fruit depends on being connected to the vine.* To put it another way, a branch bears fruit only if it has the *right connection* to the tree.

Jesus said, "I am the true vine." Out of a vine spring forth little buds called shoots. At first the shoots are just fragile green buds. Then comes the flower—the bloom ready to mature. And then comes the fruit.

It is the Creator's will that the seeds of His image planted in all of us become fruit-bearing trees. God wants all of us to become fruit-bearing branches, reflecting the character of the true vine, His Son, Jesus Christ.

Jesus says, "My Father is the vinedresser." The only thing that interests the vinedresser is fruit. He does not concern himself about the leaves or the bud, just as God is not impressed with the appearance of the foliage or the flower. He is strictly a fruit inspector. *The vinedresser has one job: to maximize the fruit of the branch.*

To ensure that every branch reaches maximum production, God prunes it. Jesus says, "Every branch that bears fruit He prunes that it may bear more fruit" (John 15:2 NKJV).

A vinedresser prunes in two ways: First, he cuts away fruitless branches that might suck sap that ought to be going to the fruitful branches. If the sap is wasted, the vine bears less fruit. Then he cuts away shoots from the fruitful branches, so that all the sap concentrates on enabling that branch to bear fruit.

God's favorite pruning knife is His Word, which Hebrews 4:12 tells us "is sharper than any two-edged sword." God uses this knife to cut and clean the branch. As you read God's Word, God cuts away the bad so it doesn't get in the way of the good, then God cuts out the good so it doesn't get in the way of the best.

This explains (at least in part) why God allows difficult times to invade our lives. Trials, troubles, and tribulations may simply be pruning shears in the hands of the divine Vinedresser, tools He uses to cut away dead wood, fruitless branches, and sap-sucking shoots so that we might bear more fruit.

I have had the privilege of spending a few minutes with the great evangelist Dr. Billy Graham. I believe he has embodied the principles found in this book and has become a winner who has influenced millions of people.

I was awed and humbled to lay hands on this mighty servant of the Lord to pray for him just before he went to preach the gospel to thirty-eight thousand people. Dr. Graham once said: "Mountaintops are for views and inspiration, but fruit is grown in the valleys."

How true. It's easy to love those who love us, but Jesus said to love our enemies. It's easy to be happy when the sun is shining; it is another to be joyful when the hail is falling, the thunder is roaring, and the lightning is crashing. Jesus said, "I have spoken these things to you so that My joy may be in you and your joy may be complete" (John 15:11). It's one thing to be at peace and calm when life feels peaceful and calm around us; it's another to be at peace when life is caving in on us. But Jesus said, "Peace I leave with you. My peace I give to you. I do not give to you as the world gives. Your heart must not be troubled or fearful" (John 14:27).

You and God: The Right Connection

How does the branch bear fruit? By trying? No. By working? No. By straining? No. The branch bears fruit simply by *abiding*. Jesus said, "He who abides in Me, and I in him, bears much fruit" (John 15:5 NKJV). What does this mean? How does one abide in Jesus? Let me suggest an analogy.

When we put a tea bag in a cup of hot water, something amazing happens to the water. As the tea bag remains, or abides in that water, the tea begins to color and flavor the water until that water begins to take on the color and the taste of the tea bag. The longer the bag abides in the water, the stronger the color and taste of the tea.

That is exactly what happens when we abide in Christ and He abides in us. The longer we abide in Christ and the deeper we go with Christ, the more the influence of Christ will pervade our lives, so that we begin to reflect His nature and His character.

The branch does not produce the fruit; it only bears the fruit. It is the vine that produces the fruit. "Abide in Me, and I in you. As the branch cannot bear fruit of itself, unless it abides in the vine, neither can you, unless you abide in Me" (John 15:4 NKJV). The branch can produce leaves, but only the vine can produce fruit.

Without the vine, the strongest branch is as helpless as the weakest branch. The most beautiful branch is as useless as the ugliest branch. The best branch is as worthless as the worst branch.

That's why Jesus went on to say, "I am the vine, you are the branches. He who abides in Me, and I in him, bears much fruit; for without Me you can do nothing" (John 15:5 NKJV). In effect, Jesus said, "I am the socket and you are the plug." Without the socket, the plug can do nothing.

Again, *it is the vine that produces the sap that enables the branch to produce the fruit.* We cannot manufacture these nine winning character traits outside of ourselves— the Spirit of God must supernaturally produce them inside of us. He does that when we abide in Christ.

But what, exactly, does it mean to abide in Christ? Jesus does not leave us wondering. Jesus tells us that abiding means, first of all, *studying the Word of God.* Jesus says, "If you abide in Me, and My words abide in you, you will ask what you desire, and it shall be done for you" (John 15:7 NKJV). When the children of God look into the Word of God and see the Son of God, they are changed by the Spirit of God into the image of God by the grace of God for the glory of God. That is what abiding is all about.

Abiding also means *doing the work of God.* Jesus said, "He who abides in Me, and I in him, bears much fruit." God is in the fruit-bearing business. That is His work; that is what He desires for us.

Third, abiding is *obeying the will of God.* Jesus said, "If you keep My commandments, you will abide in My love, just as I have kept My Father's commandments and abide in His love" (John 15:10 NKJV). When the branch rests in fellowship with the vine, it reproduces the fruit of the vine.

God in You: The Right Connection

A branch without a vine is lifeless. Because it is lifeless, it is fruitless; and because it is fruitless, it is useless. God wants you connected to Him so that He can give you the supernatural power you need to be the winner He created you to be, that you might influence others to be winners as well.

You make this connection through a personal relationship with His Son, Jesus Christ, who died on a cross and was raised from the dead so that, through faith in Him, we might be grafted as branches onto the heavenly vine and thus begin to bear the heavenly fruit of His Holy Spirit. That is the secret to being a winner who can influence anybody—the right connection.

Impressive but Dead

A Christian college in the Midwest once boasted a large, lovely oak tree in the middle of the campus. Students met and talked there, and for decades this giant tree beautified the school grounds and gave shade to thousands of students.

One day a loud crack echoed across the campus when that enormous tree crashed to the ground, broken in half. When officials examined that tree, they discovered that disease had eaten away everything but the outer trunk. Inside they found nothing but an empty shell, so when a stiff wind blew that day, that tree snapped in half and crashed to earth. It fell because it was dead. It had no root. It lacked the right connection.

Do *you* have the right connection? Are you connected with God through the only One who can make that connection—His Son, the Lord Jesus Christ? Do you have in you the indwelling Holy Spirit, who wants to bear the divine fruit of these winning qualities in your life?

If so, ask the Holy Spirit to make you into a tree that will bear fruit of blessing on all you meet. If not, I invite you to surrender your life to Jesus Christ, the true vine, who alone can make you a winner whose influence will last for all eternity.

Notes

Introduction

1. Cited by Leith Anderson, *Leadership That Works* (Minneapolis: Bethany House Publishers, 1999), 133.

2. *Bartlett's Familiar Quotations,* Justin Kaplin, ed. (Boston: Little, Brown, and Company, 1992), 231.

3. Dale Carnegie, *How to Win Friends and Influence People* (New York: Pocket Books, 1981), xvi.

Chapter 1

1. www.inspirationpoint.com/iplang.htm.

2. *Atlanta Journal* (April 1998).

3. "Alumni Association News," *UCLA Monthly* (March/April 1981): 1. This same study showed that if some "type A driven" men would hug their wives several times each day, it would increase their life spans almost two years. So, guys, start your engines.

4. Dolores Kreiger, "Therapeutic Touch: The Imprimatur of Nursing," *American Journal of Nursing* (May 1975): 784.

5. Philip Yancey, *The Jesus I Never Knew* (Grand Rapids, Mich.: Zondervan Publishing House, 1995), 171.

6. Charles Swindoll, *Dropping Your Guard* (Dallas: Word Publishing, 1983), 121.

7. *Inspiring Quotations*, compiled by Albert M. Wells Jr. (Nashville: Thomas Nelson, 1988), 119.

8. A. L. Williams, *All You Can Do Is All You Can Do but All You Can Do Is Enough!* (Nashville: Thomas Nelson, 1988), 184.

9. David Ireland with Louis Tharp Jr., *Letters to an Unborn Child* (New York: Harper & Row, 1974), 33–34.

Chapter 2

1. Sharon Begley, "A Healthy Dose of Laughter," *Newsweek* (4 October 1982): 74.

2. Charles Colson, *How Now Shall We Live?* (Wheaton, Ill.: Tyndale House, 1999), 230.

3. Paul F. Boller, *Presidential Anecdotes* (New York: Oxford University Press, 1996), 354.

4. Dale Carnegie, *How to Win Friends and Influence People* (New York: Pocket Books, 1936), 70.

5. Max Lucado, *When God Whispers Your Name* (Dallas: Word Publishing, 1994), 173.

Chapter 3

1. James Dobson, *Love for a Lifetime* (Portland, Ore.: Multnomah Press, 1987), 45.

2. Cited by Charles Swindoll, *Stress Fractures* (Portland, Ore.: Multnomah Press, 1990), 34.

3. Marco R. della Cava, "The Price of Speed," *USA Today,* 3 August 2000, 10(D).

4. Martin J. Smith, "Rushing Revolution," *Orange County Register,* 26 January 1993.

5. Joe Tevlin, "Report Says Workers Need More Family Time," *Star Tribune* (Minneapolis), 15 April 1988, 1(A).

6. "Pastoral Pressures Take Their Toll," *Pastor's Weekly Briefing* (12 February 1999): 1–2.

7. Cited by Howard Hendricks, *Standing Together* (Gresham, Ore.: Vision House Publishing, Inc., 1995), 80–81.

8. Donald Whitney, *How Can I Be Sure I'm a Christian?* (Colorado Springs, Colo.: Navpress, 1994), 80.

9. "It Is Well with My Soul," by Horatio G. Spafford, music by Phillip P. Bliss.

Chapter 4

1. John Maxwell, *The 21 Indispensable Qualities of a Leader* (Nashville: Thomas Nelson, 1999), 89.

2. *In Other Words* (summer 1977): 11.

3. Joe Torre, *Joe Torre's Ground Rules for Winners* (New York: Hyperion, 1999), 3, 8–9.

Chapter 5

1. J. B. Flower Jr., *Illustrating Great Words of the Old Testament* (Nashville: Broadman Press), 107.

2. Jill Lawrence, "Wanted: Good Citizens, Close Communities," *USA Today,* 16 January 1996, 1(A).

3. Ibid.

4. Michael LeBoeuf, *How to Win Customers and Keep Them for Life* (New York: Berkley Books, 1987), 84–85.

5. Charles Swindoll, *The Tale of the Tardy Oxcart* (Nashville: Word Publishing, 1998), 330.

6. Cited by *Christianity Today* 35, no. 10.

7. *Character Above All,* Robert A. Wilson, ed. (New York: Simon & Schuster, 1995), 219–21.

8. Steve May, *The Story File* (Peabody, Mass.: Hendriksen Publishers, 2000), 188.

Chapter 6

1. Robert E. Fitch, "The Obsolescence of Ethics," *Christianity in Crisis: A Journal of Opinion* 19, no. 19 (16 November 1959): 163–65.

2. James Madison, Federalist No. 57.

3. Forrest McDonald, *Novus Ordo Seclorum: The Intellectual Origins of the Constitution* (Lawrence, Kan.: University of Kansas Press, 1985), 72.

4. William J. Bennett, *The Death of Outrage* (Touchstone Books: 1999), 35–36.

5. Eleanor Doan, *Speaker's Sourcebook* (Grand Rapids, Mich.: Zondervan Publishing House, 1978), 114.

6. "Heroes for Today," *Reader's Digest* (2000): 13–14.

7. John Wooden, *Wooden* (New York: McGraw Hill, 1997), 93.

8. Robert Sobel, *Coolidge* (Regnery Publishers, 1998), 12–13. Italics added.

9. *The Executive Speechwriter and Newsletter* 13, no. 6.

Chapter 7

1. Cited by Pat Williams, *Go for the Magic* (Nashville: Thomas Nelson, 1998), 146.

2. *In Other Words* (fall 1999): 5–6.

3. www.ncl.org.

Chapter 8

1. Philip K. Howard, *The Death of Common Sense* (Philadelphia: Random House, 1994), 117–18.

2. John Wooden, *Wooden* (New York: McGraw Hill, 1997), 3–4.

3. Hiram W. Smith, *The 10 Natural Laws of Successful Time and Life Management* (New York: Warner Books, 1994), 46–48.

4. Michael K. Deaver, *A Different Drummer: My Thirty Years with Ronald Reagan* (New York: Harper Collins Publishers, 2001), 177.

Chapter 9

1. Peter Kim and James T. Patterson, *The Second American Revolution* (New York: William Morrow & Co., 1994), 79.

2. Charles Swindoll, *The Grace Awakening* (Dallas: Word Publishing, 1996), 280–81.

3. *Pulpit Helps* (October 1986).

4. Richard Furman, *Dr. Furman's Save Your Life Cholesterol Plan* (Nashville: Thomas Nelson, 1989), 143.

5. *USA Today,* 7 July 2000.

6. Ibid.

7. Cited by Alan Wilson, *Electric Telegraph* (Nyon, Switzerland), 3 April 2000. Italics added.

8. Vincent G. Ruggiero, *Nonsense Is Destroying America* (Nashville: Thomas Nelson, 1994), 60–61, 64, 166–67.

9. "Interview with Rubel Shelly," *Abilene Reporter-News,* 18 May 2000.

10. Pat Williams, *A Lifetime of Success* (Grand Rapids, Mich.: Fleming H. Revell, 2000), 107. Italics added.

11. Peter Drucker, *The Effective Executive* (New York: Harper & Row, 1966), viii.

12. "Wyoming Woman Accused of Starting South Dakota Wildfire," www.CNN.com.

13. Rudyard Kipling, "If," *The Best Loved Poems of the American People*, selected by Hazel Felleman (Garden City, N.Y.: Garden City Books, 1936), 65.

Chapter 10

1. Cited by Howard Hendricks, *Standing Together* (Gresham, Ore.: Vision House, 1995), 121–22.